LET'S GO!

Weekly Devotions for
Godly Competition
in the Game of Life

TRAVIS WILSON

LET'S GO!: WEEKLY DEVOTIONS FOR GODLY COMPETITION IN THE GAME OF LIFE
Copyright © 2021 by Travis Wilson
ISBN 978-1-7362277-1-8

Designed & Published by King's Daughter Publishing
Indian Trail, North Carolina 28079
www.KingsDaughterPublishing.com

Printed in the United States of America.

INTRODUCTION

The following series of devotionals are written to encourage and motivate others through real-life sports instances and the Gospel of Jesus Christ.

"Yes, I am the vine; you are the branches. Those who remain in me, and I in them, will produce much fruit. For apart from me you can do nothing" (John 15:5 NLT).

HOW TO USE THIS BOOK

Let's Go! Weekly Devotions for Godly Competition in the Game of Life contains 52 devotionals. You should read one devotional each week throughout the year.

At the end of each devotional, there is a section called "Film Study" which is followed by several scripture references. After reading the devotional, get a pen and paper, a tablet, laptop, or your notetaking method of choice. Read each scripture and make notes concerning what you believe God is saying to you personally.

Encourage a friend to also purchase this book, and take time to share your insights from the book together so you can build up one another in your faith.

"So then faith cometh by hearing, and hearing by the word of God" (Romans 10:17).

TABLE OF CONTENTS

SECOND CHANCES

LET'S·GO!
Week 1

The New England Patriots have a history of giving players like Randy Moss, Antonio Brown, Josh Gordon, Chad "Ochocinco" Johnson, and Albert Haynesworth second (and even third) chances. These athletes have encountered many troubling incidents while on other teams including drug abuse, unsportsmanlike behavior while on the field and other team distractions. Although talented, many other teams probably wouldn't have given them another shot. However, the Patriots always seem to be the one team that gives people a second chance to play the game of football. I truly believe that this is incredible—this is an example of God's grace.

What is grace? Grace is unmerited favor. Because God has allowed His one and only son, Jesus, to die for our sins, He has allowed us to have His grace. Guess what? We don't have to die to sin. All we have to do is repent to God, believe in Jesus Christ and make Him the Lord and Savior of our lives. He forgives us if we repent of our sins. Repentance means to ask God for forgiveness and turn away from sin.

God's forgiveness is amazing and I'm so thankful for it! God can forgive us so we must do the same for others. Pray for those who have wronged you (Matthew 5:44) and pray for those who continually make bad deci-

7

sions. Those who are doing wrong are really crying out for help though they may not know it.

If you are having problems forgiving others, ask God to humble you so that you can look at your own flaws, and remember that God provides you with grace. Also, pray that God will help you forgive others and He will answer your prayers (John 14:13-14). Please keep in mind that if you go to God in prayer and you are unwilling to forgive others, He will not forgive you. As a result, He will not answer your prayers (Mark 11:24-26).

Is holding a grudge worth it? No. Give everyone a second chance (and even a third or fourth chance) because God has given you chance after chance (Matthew 5:7).

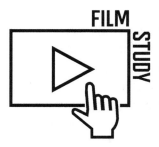

- Romans 10:9
- John 3:16-17
- Ephesians 2:8-9
- Lamentations 3:22-23
- Hebrews 8:12
- Isaiah 43:25
- Matthew 6:14
- Matthew 18:21-22

Thank God for second chances!

DREW BREES

In his junior year of high school, Drew Brees suffered a devastating injury when he tore his ACL. He went from not knowing if he was able to play football again to playing football at Purdue University. Eventually, he went to play for the San Diego Chargers, but in the last year of his contract, he dislocated his shoulder. In 2006, he ended up moving to New Orleans to play for the New Orleans Saints nearly a year after Hurricane Katrina hit. As of 2019, Brees is the number one quarterback in NFL history with 77,416 career passing yards and 547 passing touchdowns.

All of these phenomenal accomplishments happened because of God. God always takes care of His own. When you give your life to Him, He will lead you and guide you. He will give you peace and the strength to endure during the difficult moments of life. Brees could have easily given up after tearing his ACL and dislocating his shoulder. God probably told him to sign with the Saints. He could have chosen to ignore this advice—particularly after seeing how the city was devastated—but he was obedient. Look what God has done in his life! He won a Super Bowl with the Saints in 2010, broke many quarterback records, and helped many in the New Orleans community.

When tough circumstances occur or when God tells you to go some-

where or to do something uncomfortable, be obedient. As you go throughout your life, always trust in God's plan. He will make it clear when He
thinks that the time is best. Jeremiah 29:11 reminds us, *"For I know the
plans I have for you," declares the LORD, "plans to prosper you and not to
harm you, plans to give you hope and a future."*

    Sometimes God allows certain things to happen in our lives to help us
draw close to Him. In addition, He allows doors to close so that the right
door of opportunity will open at just the right time.

- Galatians 6:9
- Psalm 30:5
- Jeremiah 29:11

Always trust God's plan!

OVERCOMER

James Conner is from Erie, Pennsylvania. While in Erie, he attended McDowell Senior High School, where he played defensive lineman and running back for the Trojans football team. As a senior, he rushed for 1,680 yards and 26 touchdowns on 155 carries. The 6'1", 233 lb. running back played college football at the University of Pittsburgh from 2013-2016.

In December 2015, Conner was diagnosed with Hodgkin's Lymphoma, a type of cancer usually found in children and young adults. In 2016, a miracle happened—he overcame the cancer. Conner finished his Pitt Panther career as the ACC All-Time Touchdowns Leader with 56 career touchdowns and the ACC All-Time Rushing Touchdowns leader with 52. Also, he was named First Team All-ACC in 2016. Then, he was drafted as the 105th pick in the third round of the 2017 NFL Draft by the Pittsburgh Steelers. Currently, he is the starting running back for the Steelers. In addition, he was an AFC Pro Bowler in 2018.

One thing that God has shown through James Conner's testimony is that He is a healer! Through the pain, Conner was able to endure and overcome something as drastic as cancer.

There is someone out there who may be dealing with some sort of

11

physical ailment or disease. Please know that God is a healer. Always remember that with God, *"all things are possible to those that believe"* (Mark 9:23). Whatever the enemy meant for your bad, know that God will turn it around for your good (Genesis 50:20). Don't give up, don't lose hope, and continue to put your trust in God. Do you believe in God? Do you believe that God can do all things? Guess what? He can do all things but fail (Luke 1:37).

Someone you know may be dealing with other issues from an emotional, mental, professional, marital standpoint and even spiritual warfare but know this: God loves you! He wouldn't have allowed any difficult situation to occur in your life if He didn't think that you could handle it or ultimately conquer from it. God allows certain things to happen in your life not only to help you build endurance but to also help you grow in your faith. God knows exactly what He is doing! God is a healer.

FILM STUDY

- Romans 8:37
- Genesis 50:20
- Psalm 34:18
- Isaiah 53:5
- Mark 9:23

With God, ALL things are possible.

WEIGHTS & BAGGAGE

In order for athletes to play at peak level in their respective sports, they must eat healthy foods; work on the skill sets that relate to the sport that they play; and work on conditioning, ensuring that they will have the cardio endurance to perform at a high level. Most importantly, athletes must weight train to build muscle and to have the strength necessary to endure throughout a long season.

Life is like a long sports season that will have ups and downs. It is important that you let go of your past/baggage, especially as it pertains to previous relationships, friendships, jobs, etc. If you don't let go of the past, you will not be able to properly move forward so that you will be able to receive everything that God has for you. The enemy (the devil) wants to deter as many people as possible from pursuing a relationship with God. 1 Peter 5:8 reminds us to *"Be sober-minded; be watchful. Your adversary the devil prowls around like a roaring lion, seeking someone to devour."* God allowed that person or situation to be "the past" for a reason. Maybe that person or opportunity was not advantageous for you in that season of your life or that person or situation simply wasn't for you.

Don't allow the enemy to play tug of war with your mind. It's the first thing the enemy attacks. If you are not careful, negative thoughts lead to negative desires of the heart, which will ultimately lead to sinful actions. Guard your heart, be strong in the Lord, and do the opposite of what the enemy is enticing you to do. When Jesus was tempted by the enemy in Matthew 4:1-11, He counteracted Satan's attack with scripture. We must follow Jesus' example and memorize scripture so that we will *"not be ignorant to Satan's devices"* (2 Corinthians 2:11). Remember that we can't do this without reading and studying the bible for ourselves.

There are times when God will help you reconcile a past relationship or opportunity. Other times, God will remove people and situations from your life. Either way, God is in control and nothing can occur without His authorization. We should always remember that God doesn't make mistakes and He has a plan for all of our lives. Trust His plan and know that everything will work out in His timing. Give your past and your worries to God so that you can ultimately be free to be the man or woman that God desires you to be.

FILM STUDY

- John 8:36
- Hebrews 12:1
- Isaiah 43:18-19
- Philippians 3:13-14
- Joshua 1:8

Release the past and enjoy the future!

GAUFF
vs.
OSTAPENKO

On October 13, 2019, 15-year-old Coco Gauff became the youngest WTA singles champion when she beat 22-year-old, Jelena Ostapenko (6-3, 1-6, 6-2). With her play on the tennis court, Gauff has put the sports world on notice that despite her age, she is here to stay.

This reminds me of the story of David & Goliath in the Bible (1 Samuel 17). In this story, Saul, the first king of Israel, initially doubted David's ability to defeat Goliath because of his youth and stature. But God! He enabled David to defeat and kill Goliath with a stone and a sling and he cut Goliath's head off with Goliath's own sword (1 Samuel 17:40-50).

In life, you should never doubt yourself or think that you can't accomplish something because of a deficiency or what people may say. Know that God loves you very much and that you are *"fearfully and wonderfully made"* (Psalms 139:14). God wouldn't tell you to do anything He hasn't given you the ability to accomplish. With God, you can do all things!

- 1 Samuel 17 (entire chapter)
  - Psalms 139:14
  - Matthew 19:26
  - Isaiah 64:8
- 2 Corinthians 3:5

Never doubt yourself.

ATHLETIC PREPARATION

LET'S·GO!

Week 6

Athletes use the off-season to work on their conditioning, nutrition, and weight training. This enhances their cardiovascular endurance, improves eating habits, and builds strength in preparation for the next season. In addition, they use this time to make improvements by working on their overall skill sets. In the process of working on their games, they work on eliminating weaknesses and fine-tuning their strengths. This process will not only help athletes eliminate rust once the next season arises, but it will also help them to continue to build skills without limitations.

We all have weaknesses that we need God to help us address. But we have also been blessed with various gifts. We shouldn't find our identity in our abilities. We should walk in humility recognizing that the gifts that we have come from God. As the Body of Christ, we cannot rest on our laurels just because we are saved. No one is perfect but Jesus Christ. Therefore, we must constantly strive for excellence and growth in our relationship with Jesus Christ through prayer and studying the word of God.

We must remember that "this world is not our permanent home, we must prepare for a home to come," in other words, heaven (Hebrews

13:14). Therefore, we shouldn't focus on obtaining wealth and the plea-sures of this world in risk of totally losing our souls (Mark 8:36). God wants His people to blessed, but we should first focus on God's purpose for our lives and most importantly, the Great Commission. Matthew 28:19 tells us to *"go and make disciples of all nations, baptizing them in the name of the Father and of the Son and of the Holy Spirit, and teaching them to obey everything I have commanded you. And surely I am with you always, to the very end of the age."* As we tell others the good news of the gospel of Christ, we must not abandon maturing in our personal walk with Him. The more we allow God to help us to improve our weaknesses and strengths daily, the more we will grow to become like Christ.

FILM STUDY

- Philippians 3:14
- Hosea 10:12
- Psalms 138:6
- Matthew 28:19

Always strive for excellence and growth.

CLUTCH

Athletes like Kobe Bryant, Adam Vinatieri, David Ortiz, Michael Jordan, Tiger Woods, and Tom Brady have been known, not only for being great athletes in their respective sports but also for their ability to make big plays and be "clutch" in crucial moments to help their teams win. Their teammates, coaches, and fans expect for them to make those plays when it matters most.

Example of clutch accolades/performances:

- Kobe Bryant nailed at least 25 game-winning shots in his 20 NBA seasons. He helped the Los Angeles Lakers win five championships.
- Adam Vinatieri is generally recognized as the greatest clutch field goal kicker in NFL history. He kicked approximately 28 clutch field goals in his career in both the regular season and postseason combined. His field goals helped the New England Patriots win two Super Bowls.
- David Ortiz, former first baseman for the Boston Red Sox, hit around .800 during the 2013 World Series versus the St. Louis Cardinals. His stellar play led the team to a World Series victory. He was also named World Series MVP.
- Michael Jordan has made approximately 25 game-winning shots

in his 15-year NBA career. His ability to hit clutch shots in big moments propelled the Chicago Bulls to win six NBA championships.
- Tiger Woods has won 15 major championships during his phenomenal PGA career. An example of Woods' clutch ability was when he made a putt on 18 to force a playoff with Bob May during the 2000 PGA Championship. Woods went on to win the PGA Championship.
- Tom Brady has 45 game-winning drives, including 13 when it mattered most in the postseason. Brady led the New England Patriots to six Super Bowl wins.

God wants us to trust that He will make a way for us. He helps us during the most difficult situations of life, even when it's seems like there is nothing else to do.

God heals us emotionally, physically, mentally, and most importantly, spiritually. God is able to provide for us in every way. Trust God and His timing and that He knows what is best, why it is best, how it is best, and when it is best. He may not come when you want Him, but He is always on time. God will always come up clutch when you need Him the most.

FILM STUDY

- Hebrews 11:6
- Ephesians 3:20
- Philippians 4:19
- Habakkuk 2:3

Trust God to make a way.

THE JOY OF THE LORD IS OUR STRENGTH

O n October 3, 2019, during the Seattle Seahawks vs. St. Louis Rams game, Rams kicker, Greg Zuerlein, missed the potential game-winning field goal in the fourth quarter. The Seahawks held on for the victory, 30-29. After the missed kick, 68-year-old Seahawks head coach, Pete Carroll, ran swiftly along the sideline like a 20-year-old because of the win.

I love the energy and joy that Coach Carroll possesses during football games. You can tell that he typically doesn't allow things to bring him down. He also does a great job of encouraging his players while holding them accountable so that they can reach their full potential.

As Christians, we will suffer losses, but God promises that He will never leave us. All we have to do is go to Him in prayer and trust that He will help us to endure and overcome. We must praise God in advance for what He will do in our lives. We must also seek Him in prayer. When we do, we will experience the joy that only God gives. When we experience God's joy in our lives, we will also receive His strength to endure and overcome any situation.

No matter what we face, we know that God has a plan for our lives. We can be confident that God can give us the joy that we need if we go to Him, seek Him first, and trust Him. The joy of The Lord is our strength.

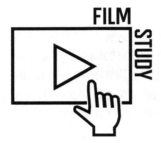

FILM STUDY

- Psalm 16:11
- Psalm 100
- Nehemiah 8:10
- Philippians 4:6-7
- 1 Thessalonians 5:16

Learn to praise God in advance.

LET'S·GO!
⑳
Week 9

DOUBLE TEAMED

Sometimes in basketball and football, athletes (specifically star players) get "doubled teamed" on offense by their opponents because the opposing players and coaches respect the star players' ability to dominate the game offensively.

Have you ever felt like you have faced obstacle after obstacle—double teamed by problems—and you wonder if there will be any relief?

God loves you and has a plan for your life. Know that the enemy doesn't mess with people that are not a threat to his kingdom. God's people are always a threat to the enemy because they interrupt his plans of trying to destroy them or others by causing them to sin. Satan's job is to destroy many people and keep others from seeking God. We can overcome the enemy's tactics by being strong in the Lord, growing in our relationship with God, and by loving God and others. When you pass every test that Satan brings your way, he will come even harder the next time by attacking you with legions (many) of demons, Satan's fallen angels. These fallen angels are under the control of Satan to tempt people to do evil. God kicked Satan out of heaven because of his rebellion (Ezekiel 28). Now, Satan is mad and is willing to do whatever it takes to attack God's people and the things of God. Remember that *"no weapon formed against you will prosper"* as it says in Isaiah 54:17.

Be strong in the Lord, live for Him, obey Him, love Him, and read and study the bible so that you can truly grow in God daily while understanding the enemy's tactics. With God on your side, you can't lose. Even when you are double teamed, you can only win.

FILM

STUDY

- Isaiah 54:17
- 1 John 4:4
- Ephesians 6:10-11
- James 4:7
- 2 Corinthians 5:11
- Matthew 8:28-34
- 2 Timothy 3:12

Satan's weapons will never succeed.

MAN OF GOD

In 2019, the NFL fined Demario Davis, linebacker for the New Orleans Saints, for wearing a "Man of God" headband during the Week 3 match-up versus the Seattle Seahawks. He was fined because his headband was a uniform violation. Davis appealed the fine and won. Not only did he win, but he used the money he received to benefit a hospital in Jackson, Mississippi.

As Christians, we must understand that we will face persecution for being men and women of God. However, we must also understand the importance of being strong in the Lord because *"those who endure to the end will be saved"* (Matthew 24:13). Whenever the enemy tries to negatively affect you, God will turn it around for your good so that He will receive the glory.

Davis could have easily kept the money since he won the fine appeal, but he apparently understood the principle of Luke 12:48: *"To whom much is given, much is required."* We all must understand that we are blessed to be a blessing to others.

FILM STUDY

- Philippians 2:9-11
- Genesis 50:20
- Isaiah 54:17
- Acts 20:35
- 1 Peter 3:15
- Luke 12:48

God turns persecution around for our good.

LET YOUR 'YES' BE 'YES' AND YOUR 'NO' BE 'NO'

I n 2019, Marcus Morris made a verbal commitment to the San Antonio Spurs to join the team but ultimately signed with the New York Knicks. Four years earlier, during the summer of 2015, DeAndre Jordan verbally committed to join the Dallas Mavericks but ultimately decided to re-sign with the Los Angeles Clippers.

The purpose of this example is not to condemn Morris or Jordan. It is to simply help us, especially as Christians, to understand the importance of keeping our word and avoid making promises that we can't keep.

Perhaps there have been times when you made a promise to attend an event or provide a service to someone but there was truly a change of plans. But there have also been times when we make promises to do something but knew in the first place that we weren't going to do it. Sometimes in this situation, people say that they are going to "pray about it," but that is their way of avoiding the commitment instead of politely saying "no" (some really do pray about it). We are supposed to "seek God in all of our ways and He will direct our paths" as Proverbs 3:5-6 says. If we tell someone that we are going to pray about a certain situation then we must truly pray about it. It is imperative that we don't make a mockery out of God by saying that we are going to pray about something that we truly weren't going to pray about in the first place.

It is so important for us to always walk with integrity. If we don't know what to do so or say—especially as it pertains to making decisions—we should definitely ask God for clarity and He will lead us and help us with what to say or do. God wants to be a part of every aspect of our lives. Remember, people are always watching the way that we as Christians live. Therefore, we must be an example of Jesus Christ everywhere we go. Keeping our promises is one way to do so.

FILM STUDY

- Matthew 5:37
- Romans 14:16
- Proverbs 3:5-6
- 1 Timothy 4:12

Never make promises you can't keep.

FINDING IDENTITY

Cooper Kupp hails from Yakima, Washington. He attended Davis High School where he was a two-sport athlete in football and basketball. The 6'2" wide receiver dominated on the football field at Eastern Washington University. He finished his college career with 73 career receptions for 6,464 yards and 73 touchdowns. Kupp accomplished a great deal as an Eastern Washington Eagle. He was a four-time Consensus First Team FCS All-American, a 2013 Jerry Rice Award Winner for the top freshman in the FCS, 2015 & 2016 FCS ADA National Offensive Player of the Year, and many more. After a stellar college football career, Kupp was drafted 69th overall in the third round of the 2017 NFL Draft by the Los Angeles Rams.

Kupp, who is considered a Christian, was quoted as saying, "Knowing where your identity is and knowing that as much as I want to be a football player and I strive to be that, I'm so much more than that.This life is temporary but there's such things ahead. No matter what the naysayers say, no matter what anyone tells me, I know that my identity is in Christ and nothing can take me off that."

As Christians, we must remember that we represent God everywhere we go. 1 Timothy 4:12 reminds us, *"Don't let anyone think less of you because you are young. Be an example to all believers in what you say, in the way you live, in your love, your faith, and your purity."*

Regardless of your profession or your race, if you are a Christian, nothing trumps that. We must remember that we are Christians first. No matter the situation, we must always take a Christian approach in every circumstance by being an example of Jesus. This means that we must glorify God in our actions, thoughts, speech, love, and faith.

Find your identity in Jesus Christ. Don't allow your economic status, occupation, fame, fortune, or anything else to determine your worth. When you find your identity in Christ, nothing, or no one should cause you to lose your joy, peace, praise, worship, etc. Find your identity in Jesus Christ and in Him alone.

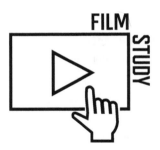

FILM STUDY

- 1 Peter 2:9-10
- Galatians 2:20

You represent Christ everywhere you go.

LET'S·GO!
②⓪ ②①
Week 13

THE VERSATILE QUARTERBACK

Taysom Hill is the youngest of four siblings. He is from Pocatello, Idaho where he lettered in football, basketball, and track at Highland High School. After high school, he went on to play college football at Brigham Young University. He finished his BYU career as the school's career leader in quarterback rushing yards and fifth overall in career rushing yards with 2,815. In addition, Hill was a two-time Davey O'Brien and Walter Camp Award watch list honoree.

Then, he was undrafted in the 2017 NFL Draft, but signed with the Green Bay Packers as a free agent. At the conclusion of the preseason, he was released by the Packers. Later, he was claimed off of waivers by the New Orleans Saints. Since arriving to New Orleans, Taysom Hill has been a great contributor to the Saints organization. He literally does it all for the team (well, almost everything). Not only does he throw the football at the quarterback position but he also rushes and catches the football as well. Hill even makes plays on special teams. He brings an added dimension to not only the Saints organization but to the NFL as a whole with his versatile playmaking ability.

It reminds me of how good God is and how He can do it ALL! He is our creator, provider, forgiver, father, doctor, lawyer, sustainer, and so much more. He is omnipresent, meaning He is everywhere. God is consistent and He never changes. Hebrews 13:8 reminds us that *Jesus Christ is the same yesterday, today, and forever.*"

We may be faced with trials and tribulations but we can be reminded that God will be there for His people. Always trust Him and use the Word of God as a resource to cling to during the good and difficult moments of life. God is our everything. He can do all things but fail.

FILM STUDY

- Matthew 19:26
- Luke 1:37
- Ephesians 3:20
- Deuteronomy 31:6
- Hebrews 13:5

God is our resource for everything we need.

THE UNSELFISHNESS OF COACH TONY BENNETT

Coach Anthony "Tony" Bennett is originally from Clintonville, Wisconsin. Bennett is currently the Head Coach of the University of Virginia men's basketball team. He has been coaching the Cavaliers since 2009. Before blowing the whistle at UVA, he had a long playing career. Bennett played college hoops at the University of Wisconsin–Green Bay (1988-1992). Then, he was the point guard for the NBA's Charlotte Hornets from 1992-1995. He finished his playing career with the North Harbour Vikings in New Zealand and the Sydney Kings in Australia, respectively.

Coach Bennett began his coaching career with the North Harbour Vikings. In 1999, Bennett had an opportunity to become an assistant coach in his home state with the University of Wisconsin Badgers, where he served until 2003. After his stint with the Badgers, he moved on to the Pacific 12 Conference then the Pacific 10 Conference as an Assistant Coach for the Washington State Cougars' men's basketball team. During his tenure, he was promoted from Assistant to Associate to Head Coach. The team had great success under his leadership. Bennett led the 2006-07 Cougars to a 26-8 record, then followed up with 26-9 record the next season. After struggling during the 2008-09 season with a 17-16 record, Bennett had an opportunity to be the head man for the University of Virginia.

Since coaching UVA in 2009, the Cavaliers have won four ACC regular season championships, two ACC Tournament championships, and a National Championship in 2019. Because of his team's success at Washington State and Virginia, Coach Bennett has been nationally recognized for his leadership. He was named Pac-10 Coach of the Year in 2007, AP & Naismith Coach of the Year twice in 2007 and 2018, ACC Coach of the Year in 2014, 2015, 2018, and 2019 among other accolades.

While Bennett has had much success as a head coach in college basketball, his most important and greatest accomplishment is becoming a Christian. I love the way that he carries himself as a Christian. He has a certain calmness about himself that is evident. His teams always seem to exhibit a certain level of class and professionalism so noticeable that it is clear they follow his lead.

Coach Tony Bennett turned down a raise that was offered to him in 2019. He requested that the money that was offered to him instead be used to give his coaching staff raises and enhance other athletic programs. Bennett said in an article released by UVA,"I have more than enough, and if there are ways that this can help out the athletic department, the other programs and coaches, by not tying up so much [in men's basketball], that's my desire."

This is a great act of selflessness, contentment, thankfulness, and humility. Be thankful and content for all the things that God has done in your life without being greedy and complaining. Help those need help whether financially, providing resources (food, water, and clothing), through encouragement, etc.

Acts 20:35 reminds us that *It is better to give than receive.* We all are blessed in so many ways. It is important for us to remember that there are many individuals who are dealing with a lot worse than we are. Always remember that we are blessed to be a blessing to those who are in need.

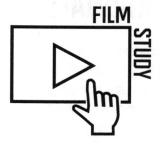

- Proverbs 22:1
- Hebrews 13:5
- 1 Corinthians 6:9-10
- Philippians 2:3-4
- 2 Corinthians 9:7-15
- Matthew 25:40-45

We are blessed to be a blessing.

LET'S·GO!
Week 15

2019 MLB CHAMPS WASHINGTON NATIONALS

One night, I watched SportsCenter and noticed how the Washington Nationals started 19-31 through their first 50 games. At the beginning of the 2019 season, they had some ups and downs, but they finished the season with a 93-69 regular season record. They were even down in every series in the playoffs. Then, the Nationals made it to the World Series vs. the Houston Astros. After being up 2-0 in the series, they were down 3-2 after five games and then won two straight games to win the World Series.

With their slow start, they could have easily given up but thankfully, there are 162 games in a MLB season. Even though they had a rough beginning, they stuck together and rallied around one another. As a result, they won when it mattered most, in the World Series.

You may be facing trial after trial, struggle after struggle and you may be wondering when you are going to catch a break. You may see others being blessed who seem to have everything that they want but you are probably thinking, "What about me?" Know that if God has allowed you to live for another day, you are blessed. If He has blessed you with shelter, food, clothes, you are blessed. If you have a job, you are blessed. If your bills are paid, you are blessed.

Stop comparing yourself to others. God has created us all with differences and everyone is in different stages in their walk with God. Others who are not saved may have everything that they desire, but they don't have the most important person in their lives—Jesus Christ. So, it is safe to say that the enemy is allowing them to have what they have to make them think that it is God blessing them with those things so that they can continue to live in sin. *"For what shall it profit a man, if he shall gain the whole world, and lose his own soul?"* (Luke 8:36) You may not have everything that you want but know that God will supply your needs and bless you in His timing. He knows what you need, when you need it, how you need it, and why you need it.

Through your trials and sufferings, God is able to build character, patience, and faith within you so that you can grow to be the man or woman that He has designed you to be. That is also when God can and will show Himself strong in your life so that He will get the glory from your life. As you grow in Him, He can prepare you for what He has for you. Think about it this way: if you get what you desire or what He has for you right off the bat without waiting for His timing or without suffering, how would you be able to build character and grow to be like Jesus Christ? Jesus suffered while here on this Earth, so what makes you think that you won't as a Christian? It is so important for us as Christians to wait on God's timing and understand that He is perfect and knows best. Since God is perfect and knows what is best, you can be sure to know that He doesn't make mistakes.

Everything that He does is for a reason. Be content in whatever situation that you are in. Seek God first in your life, pray, and trust that God will do the rest. One day, *"the first will be last and the last will be first"* (Matthews 20:16).

- Ecclesiastes 3:1
- Psalms 37:4
- Luke 8:36
- James 1:2-4

God will bless us in His perfect timing.

YOU ARE NOT ALONE

Boxing, golf, bowling, tennis, and UFC are primarily one-on-one sports in which athletes must rely on their training, preparation (offseason/in-season), and mentality in order to press through and win. This is very different from team sports like football, volleyball, lacrosse, and basketball which require an athlete to rely on his/her own ability and instincts and his/her teammates' ability and instincts to reach that common goal of winning.

- Have you ever found yourself in a situation where you felt alone?
- Have you been sad after someone who is close to you passed away?
- Have you ever felt like everyone is turning their backs on you?
- Have you ever felt alone and betrayed after your best friend has done you wrong?
- Have you ever felt betrayed and alone after your boyfriend/girl-friend or spouse has cheated on you?
- Have you ever felt alone while in prison or do you know someone who is in prison and wondering when they will be released?
- Have you or a loved one been ill and wonder if or when God will heal?

- Have you ever been homeless and wondered if God was going to supply your needs?
- Have you been single for a long period of time and you've been constantly praying and asking God to bring a man or woman of God into your life?

Unlike one-on-one sports, you are never alone with God on your side. God loves you because He is love! God sees all and knows all that you are going through because He is omnipresent and all-knowing. Since God is all knowing and omnipresent, nothing can be hidden from Him.

God oftentimes allows things to happen in your life so that you can draw closer to Him, to help build your character and faith, and to get the glory out of your life. God wants us to trust Him even in our darkest moments. It is often in the difficult moments of life that God shows Himself strong. But we must realize how important it is to have faith because without it, *"it is impossible to please God"* (Hebrews 11:6).

Faith unlocks the door for God to bless you and work in your life. God will take care of your needs. You don't have to be depressed. God will give you peace and strength. It is so important to seek Him in prayer, read/study His word, and seek godly counsel. You are not alone, God loves you. Allow God to work in your life. He knows what He is doing.

FILM STUDY

- Hebrews 13:6
- 1 John 4:8
- James 4:8
- 1 Peter 5:7
- Matthew 11:28-30
- Hebrews 11:6
- Deuteronomy 31:6

God knows everything you're going through.

BLESSED TO BE A BLESSING

Philanthropy is common to athletes. Philanthropic efforts include giving back to their communities by helping those who are in need financially, physically, mentally, etc. One thing that we forget sometimes is that some athletes didn't grow up in wealthy households. Some grew up in single parent households or had parents who faced financial difficulty or were even homeless. Some of them may have suffered with physical challenges or have loved ones who did. In addition, we must remember that they are not superhuman. They are people who have faced difficult circumstances in life just like you and I.

In spite of everything that some athletes have gone through, by the grace of God they are able to use those experiences as motivation to not only enhance their lives but also their family's lives. After reaching their childhood dream of playing collegiate and/or professional sports, most athletes have remembered their personal experiences and have used those experiences to help others reach their goals and lend a hand to those who are less fortunate.

In 2015, after Hurricane Harvey, J.J. Watt, newly-acquired defensive end for the Arizona Cardinals, donated and helped those hurricane victims in Houston. LeBron James, small forward for the Los Angeles Lakers, has been extremely philanthropic throughout his NBA career. He has helped so many by donating through his LeBron James Family Foundation, opening his IPROMISE School for grades 1-8, and he has even helped individuals go to college. Michael Jordan opened the Novant Health Michael Jordan Family Medical Clinic to provide healthcare to those who have little to no health insurance.

These are only few great examples of athletes who have used their resources to bless others. Like these athletes, it is so important to understand how blessed we are, whether we have a lot or little. Be content and thankful for what God has done in your life. Give to those who are less fortunate whether if it is through money, food, clothing/shoes, time, support/encouragement, etc. If we see someone who is homeless on the side of the road and you lend money to them, don't worry about what they do with it. Do the right thing and give. If they use the money for what they are not supposed to do, allow that to be between them and God. Always use discernment and allow God to lead you.

We understand that God just doesn't bless us for our own gain, but He blesses us to be a blessing in the lives of others.

FILM STUDY

- Acts 20:35
- Luke 12:48

Use your resources to bless others.

43

PHILLIP LINDSAY

LET'S·GO!
Week 18

Phillip Lindsay finished his University of Colorado career as the program's all-time leader in all-purpose yards (5,926) and yards from scrimmage (4,849). In 2018, he was undrafted to the NFL and was signed by the Denver Broncos. He had a great rookie year with many accolades. Lindsey ranked first in franchise history and second all-time for an undrafted rookie with 1,037 rushing yards. In addition, he rushed for 9 touchdowns. He became the first undrafted player in NFL history to surpass 100 yards from scrimmage in each of his first two NFL games. He was also the first undrafted offensive rookie in NFL history to be selected to the Pro Bowl.

I'm sure that Phillip Lindsey's dream was to play in the NFL. He could have easily given up after being overlooked in the draft, but he ended up making the Broncos team out of training camp. He could have thought that he was unqualified to be on an NFL team because he was undrafted and stood only 5'8" but he never gave up.

Don't allow anyone to think any less of you because of your circumstances. You are not qualified by people but you are qualified by God. If you have a desire, a dream, and a passion to do something, seek God about it in prayer, work hard, have faith and trust that He will make a way and open the door for you.

- 2 Corinthians 3:5
- Matthew 19:30
- Jeremiah 29:11

Only God, not people, can qualify you.

OBEDIENCE WHEN YOU OR PEOPLE DON'T UNDERSTAND

What does "prime" mean as it pertains to sports? "Prime" in sports mean seasons close or somewhat close to the peak of an athlete's career. The prime in an athlete's career doesn't typically last long. When it occurs, they must take full advantage of it by reaching their full potential and playing at a high level.

Many great athletes like Luke Kuechly (football), Bjorn Borg (tennis), and Ken Dryden (hockey), have retired in their primes or possibly earlier than people would have liked or expected. Reasons include the accumulation of injuries throughout the years, a lack of passion for the sport, or to spend more time with their families, etc.

Sometimes people will make decisions that we may not understand just like others may not understand certain decisions that we make. It is important for us as Christians to constantly grow in our relationship with God. As we grow, we must stay in tune with Him by willingly listening when He speaks to us. Remember that God speaks in a small still voice (1 Kings 19:12).

There are many times as Christians when God will instruct us to do something that we may not understand initially but we certainly will later. We must always listen to God because He is our Father. He knows best. He has a plan and a purpose for our lives and *"He knows the end from the beginning"* (Isaiah 46:10). Many people will not understand the decisions that we make even if we are led by God. That is why we shouldn't worry about other individuals' opinions. Obedience and trust in God are important keys for God to bless us and show Himself strong in our lives so that He will be glorified.

FILM STUDY

- Isaiah 46:10
- 1 Samuel 15:22
- Jeremiah 29:11
- Galatians 1:10

Obey God even if you don't understand.

N.G.A.
NO GUILT
ALLOWED

In March 2016, University of Alabama wide receiver Henry Ruggs, III lost his close friend, Rod Scott, due to head injuries sustained in a car accident. His friend and some others were on their way to attend a state playoff basketball game in Birmingham, Alabama. Ruggs III had planned to travel with the group, but couldn't because he was sick with the flu. Ruggs III and Scott had played high school basketball together. They were so close that Scott was the reason that Ruggs had eventually taken football seriously and why he ultimately decided to attend the University of Alabama. Rod Scott saw the football talent that Henry Ruggs III exhibited.

After the death of his friend, Ruggs III felt guilty because he knew that if he was with his friends that day, Scott would have let him drive. One thing that we must understand is that everything happens for a reason. If Ruggs III had been in the car that day, there is a chance that he wouldn't be here today excelling on the football field.

God "sees the end from the beginning" and has a plan for everything. There are many times in life when we have done something that we regret and we may feel responsible for it. Because of God allowing His Son, Jesus to die for us, we have His grace. Because we have God's grace, believers in Jesus don't have to live in guilt or condemnation.

If you have made a mistake, know that God loves you and repent. If you know someone who has made a mistake, show the love of Jesus, speak the truth in love to them, and pray for them. Let go of the past and remember N.G.A...."No Guilt Allowed."

- Romans 8:1
- Ephesians 2:8-10
- Titus 3:6
- Philippians 3:13

God's grace covers our regrets.

LEADING THE PACK

When you think of leadership, what do you think of?

- A leader who leads vocally and teaches.
- A leader who leads by example on and off the field and/or court.
- A leader who has an incredible work ethic.
- A leader of men or women who teaches players right from wrong on and off the court or field from a moral standpoint.
- A leader who not only teaches the importance of athletics, but also academics.
- One who encourages and/or motivates
- One who disciplines, brings the best out of others, and demands respect.
- One who not only coaches from an X's and O's standpoint and focuses on wins or losses, but one who truly cares for his or her teammates, players, and staff in every aspect of life.
- One who knows how to respectfully communicate with others.
- One who knows when to criticize, encourage, or embrace those around him or her.
- Someone who remains positive in spite of any circumstance (good or bad).

- One who sacrifices for the betterment of the team.
- A leader who offers wise advice with humility.
- A leader who knows when to speak and when to listen.

Leadership is a key component for a team to build camaraderie, reach their full potential as a team, meet their team goals, and win!

Leadership is not only important in sports, but it is important in all areas of life. For example, as a manager on your job, as a father or husband, or as a pastor in and out of the church. Without great leadership, the group, team, church, staff, nation, or family will be in turmoil. Great leadership will help things stay afloat even when things don't go right. It is so important to trust and believe that God will make a way and provide. Great leadership focuses on the task at hand, making sure that goals are met, and that purpose is being fulfilled with the Lord at the forefront. In addition, phenomenal leaders care for the needs of the people they lead.

God is the best leader that one can ever have. He sacrificed by allowing His Own Son, Jesus to die for our sins.

God supplies all our needs; all we must do is trust in Him and live for Him.

God loves us despite us. He offers grace to us.

He offers wisdom to those who ask for it (James 1:5).

He forgives (1 John 1:9).

He loves us because He is love (1 John 4:8).

He listens to those who does His Will (John 9:27).

Jesus gives the Holy Spirit to those who are saved to lead us and guide us in our everyday life (John 14:15-31).

God provides us with the Bible to order our every step and help us to be like Jesus Christ in this journey called "life." (Psalms 119:105)

Leadership is a necessity for growth to happen spiritually, professionally, financially, emotionally, mentally, etc. If God has called you to lead, lead well and do all things with God as the foundation of your life and watch how God will work.

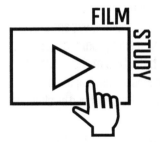

- Proverbs 11:14
- Proverbs 15:22
- Proverbs 22:6
- Hosea 4:6
- Psalms 119:105
- John 14:26

God is the best leader we could ever have.

HUMILITY THROUGH THE STRUGGLE

Carmelo Anthony should be a future NBA Hall of Famer in my opinion. Anthony is a 10-time All Star, 2012-2013 scoring champion, and a six-time All-NBA recipient who averaged nearly 24 points per game. After being the third overall pick in the 2003 NBA Draft, he was the star and number one offensive option for the Denver Nuggets and the New York Knicks. After his stint with the Knicks ended, things began to change in his career. He was traded to multiple teams where he was no longer the number one option including the Oklahoma City Thunder and the Houston Rockets (he played only ten games with the Rockets). Then, he was traded to the Chicago Bulls where he was ultimately released before playing a single game.

After being released by the Bulls, he was out of the NBA for a year because no one would sign him. It was believed that teams were hesitant to sign him because of his isolation playing style that limits ball movement. Because of his playing style, they thought that he wouldn't be a good fit. Anthony stated in an interview with ESPN's Rachel Nichols that he heard people saying that he was "selfish," a "bad teammate," and a "bad locker room guy."

I truly believe that Anthony had a hard time being a third or fourth option in an offense with the Thunder and Rockets especially after being the number one option for so many years. I'm sure that his hiatus from the NBA was difficult and unusual that a team didn't add him to their roster. After a period of time of not getting signed, he considered retiring from the NBA. However, his hiatus from the game of basketball humbled him and he not only grew mentally but he also grew overall as a person.

After a year off, the Portland Trail Blazers gave him the opportunity to play. Since signing with the Trail Blazers, he has been a phenomenal fit for the team. Carmelo Anthony has been in a great position where he can start and help their star guards, Damian Lillard and CJ McCollum, with his perimeter scoring and experience. He not only received an opportunity to play in the NBA again, he is playing well and was once named Western Conference Player of the Week. Maybe he needed that time away to help humble him and help him to grow individually as a basketball player and an individual.

Has there ever been a point in your life where you've been successful?

Has there ever been a point in your life where everything has begun to fall into place in your life?

Has there ever been a point in your life where you have received fame and fortune because of your talent but you forget that God is number one and He is the One who gave you the talent in the first place?

Has there been a point in your life where you became a little arrogant because of your success?

Has there ever been a point in your life where things have hit rock bottom after they were going so well?

God wants His children to be blessed. 3 John 1:2 says, *"Beloved, I pray that you may prosper in all things and be in health, just as your soul prospers."* Although God wants us to be blessed, He also wants us to walk in humility, recognizing that we are nothing without Him. There are times in our lives when we begin "feeling" ourselves a little bit and if we are not careful, we will find ourselves not seeking God and leaning on Him like we should. During those times, God will allow certain things to happen in our lives to humble us and help us draw close to Him so that we can ultimately be more like Him.

When we seek God first in our lives and walk in humility, recognizing that we can't live this life without Him, it opens up the door for God to bless us tremendously. Praise God for who He is and what He's done.

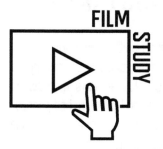

FILM STUDY

- John 10:10
- James 4:6
- Psalm 138:6
- 1 Peter 2:9

We are nothing without God.

YOU ARE NOT YOUR MISTAKES

After a spectacular pass to Malik Turner on 3rd and 16 with over 8 minutes left in overtime vs. the San Francisco 49ers during the 2019 season, Seattle Seahawks QB Russell Wilson threw an unusual interception with 5:46 left in the period.The 49ers had possession of the football and were stopped in field goal range. Then, Chase McLaughlin, kicker for the 49ers who made his first three kicks, had an opportunity to be the hero and win the game, but from 47 yards with 3:06 left, he missed the kick. This gave Wilson another opportunity to lead the Seahawks down the field for a potential game-winning drive. On 3rd and 3 with over a minute left in the game, Wilson made a big time play with a 21-yard run. The Seahawks allowed time to go down and clocked it (stopped the clock by spiking the ball to the ground). With 4 seconds remaining, their kicker, Jason Myers hit the game winning kick to win the game for Seattle. The final score was 27-24, leading to the 49ers first loss in the 2019 season.

Russell Wilson does a terrific job of remaining positive, resilient, and encouraging during the difficult and great moments of the game. He seems to have a peace about him and doesn't get rattled if he or someone else on offense turns over the ball. He moves on to the next play and if an opportunity presents itself to get the ball back, most times he makes the clutch play to help his team win. During the Monday Night Football game his resolve showed. After he threw the interception earlier in the overtime period, he came back and made the plays necessary to put the Seahawks in position to make the game-winning field goal.

In this journey called life, we all make mistakes. Romans 6:23 says, *"For all have sinned, and come short of the glory of God."* The question is how are we responding to the mistakes that we have made?

Do we overlook our sins and blame others for our sins as a result?

Do we avoid taking responsibility for the sins that we commit without repentance?

After sinning, do we walk in guilt and allow the enemy to make us think that our mistake defines us?

Or do we allow the Holy Spirit to help us recognize when we fall short, prompting us to ask God to forgive us with a repentant heart?

It is important for us to humble ourselves and make the latter our choice. We must recognize and acknowledge what we have done and soften our hearts to hear from God and repent of our sins.

God is a loving and forgiving God who gives us another chance. You don't have to feel down and live in guilt for the mistakes you've made. God allowed His Son Jesus to die for us and our sins which enables us to believe in Jesus Christ and experience God's grace. What is grace? Grace is God's free and unmerited favor toward sinful humanity. God is so good! Do we deserve God's grace? No. Should we take advantage of God's grace by sinning purposely and then asking God for forgiveness because we know that He will forgive? No.

Always remember that God looks at our heart and knows the true intentions of our hearts. If we have the grace of God, we can live righteously for Him knowing that He is faithful to forgive us when we mess up. If you sin, allow God to touch your heart through the Holy Spirit (for those who are saved), acknowledge what you have done wrong, repent of your sins, and move forward living the life that God desires for you to live through His Word. God loves you and He allowed His son Jesus to die for you. You are not your mistakes.

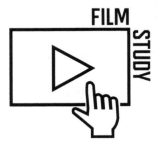

FILM STUDY

- John 3:16-17
- Ephesians 2:8
- Romans 6:15-16
- 1 John 1:9
- Hebrews 8:12

Your mistakes do not define you. God does.

HOW DO YOU RESPOND TO CRITICISM?

On November 25, 2019, the Philadelphia 76ers played the Toronto Raptors in Toronto. The 76ers lost 101-96. Despite having 13 rebounds, the 76ers best player, Joel Embiid, probably had his worst game as a NBA player with 0 points and 4 turnovers. He was 0-11 from the field, 0-4 from the three-point line, and 0-3 from the free throw line in 32 minutes of play. After, he received plenty of criticism for his lack of aggression and not using his 7'0, 280-pound frame to consistently dominate in the paint instead of taking a lot of perimeter shots (despite having the skill set to do so).

Two nights later, the 76ers played against the Sacramento Kings. Embiid bounced back with a 33 point, 16 rebound performance. He finished 10-19 from the field and 12-14 from the free throw line in 32 minutes.

On December 10, 2019, the Philadelphia 76ers played the Denver Nuggets, winning the game 97-92. Embiid finished this game with 22 points, 10 rebounds, and 6 assists. There are many who think that this stat line is phenomenal. There are also many who have played in the NBA and analyze the game of basketball for a living who truly believe that a person with Embiid's ability and size should dominate on the basketball court with consistency and more scoring in the post. After the game on Inside the NBA, Hall of Famers Charles Barkley (former power forward for the

Philadelphia 76ers, Phoenix Suns, and Houston Rockets) and Shaquille O'Neal (former center for the Orlando Magic, Los Angeles Lakers, Miami Heat, and others) followed this sentiment. Shaq stated Embiid wasn't playing well. Shaq wasn't saying that in an envious or negative way but he wanted to provide constructive criticism because he sees greatness in him. Shaquille O' Neal was speaking from experience. He was widely recognized as the most dominant force in NBA history because of his size and agility. He also stated, "22 points is okay but it isn't great; if you have the potential to be a great player, we expect great things." Charles Barkley began talking about matchups and when it comes to huge matchups like it was that night between Joel Embiid and another great center who plays for the Nuggets, Nikola Jokic, he noted that Embiid needed to be ready to play and dominate.

After these critical comments, the media began to ask Embiid for his opinion on what Shaq and Barkley said. Embiid understood and respected what they were saying because they had already experienced playing basketball at a high level. He recognized that he needed to play better and with more consistency. Two nights later, Embiid led the 76ers to a huge win vs. Boston, 115-109. He responded to the criticism dominating inside and outside of the paint with 38 points, 13 rebounds, and 6 assists. He finished 12-21 from the field and he played with a lot of aggression by shooting 14 free throws, making 12 of them.

One thing that we must realize is that there will be people who are going on hate on us because of the abilities that God has given us. They may be jealous of how God has blessed us and want what we have. But there are also people that God has placed in our lives who pray for us and see greatness in us. Like Shaquille O'Neal and Charles Barkley, they see greatness in us and offer us constructive criticism because they love us and want to bring the best out of us.

Every day, God wants us to grow in our relationship with Him. The ways to do so is through prayer and reading and studying God's word. As we grow in our relationship with God, we will begin recognizing who Jesus is and how He lived so that we can be more like Him. In order for us to truly grow in Jesus Christ, we must look at ourselves in the mirror and humbly and honestly evaluate our strengths and weaknesses. In addition, we must allow the Holy Spirit to lead us. How can we truly grow in every area of life if we don't humble ourselves enough to recognize and evaluate the areas where we are weak or strong?

As we honestly self-evaluate, we shouldn't take offense to the criticism given by others. Rather, criticism should confirm what the Holy Spirit has already said. Please be sure to use discernment on what criticism/encouragement is from God. If it is negative feedback, the enemy may also be trying to use certain people to give you as a form of discouragement or to cause you to think negatively about yourself. 1 John 4:1 encourages us to *"test the spirit by the spirit and see if it is of God."*

There are many times when God will allow certain things to happen in our lives as a form of discipline. God disciplines us because He loves us, He wants us to draw close to Him and grow in Him, and He knows what is best for us.

How do we respond to criticism? Walk in humility, use discernment, and grow. Most importantly, grow in God.

FILM STUDY

- 1 John 4:1
- Proverbs 12:1
- Proverbs 12:6

Criticism can help us grow if we use it right.

LET'S·GO!
Week 25

CRAWL BEFORE YOU WALK

In his first three NFL seasons out of the University of California, Aaron Rodgers was a backup quarterback for the Green Bay Packers behind star quarterback and Hall of Famer, Brett Favre. During those years, I'm sure that he wanted to start but he was able to learn a great deal from Favre. Brett Favre certainly wouldn't be a bad person to learn from. Favre finished his career as an 11-time Pro Bowler, a three time MVP, and a Super Bowl Champion who has thrown for 71,838 career yards and 508 career touchdowns.

In 2008, Brett Favre was traded to the New York Jets. From that point, the reserve quarterback, Aaron Rodgers had his opportunity to lead the Pack. Since starting, Rodgers has risen to the occasion. In 2011, he led the Packers as they won Super Bowl XLV and was named the Super Bowl MVP.

Rodgers is a three-time NFL MVP, a nine-time Pro Bowler, and a three-time All Pro. It is safe to say that he has been able to take full advantage of his opportunity. Although he wasn't able to start at the beginning of his career, he was able to learn and grow to be the best NFL quarterback that he can possibly be.

Have you ever experienced small beginnings?

Have you ever suffered, wondering when God would bring you into a better situation?

Have you been on your job for a long period of time, have excelled tremendously and you wonder if or when you will be promoted?

If any of these situations describes you or someone else that you know, please know that God has a plan for your life. Just as the earth's seasons change, God allows us to go through various seasons in our lives. Through those seasons, He will help us to know how to endure various circumstances as we grow in our relationship with Him and allow Him to take full control of our lives. As we allow God to take full control of our lives, we can trust that He knows what is best for us.

Often, God allows us to face trials and tribulations or desires that we wait for a breakthrough because He wants our faith and our reliance on Him to increase. His goal is always for us to grow in our relationship with Him and ultimately become more like Christ.

You may be thinking, "I have been looking to grow in God. I have been trusting God. I have been patient. I have been living holy and right. I have been single for so long. When is my husband or wife coming?" There may be many questions that enter your mind. I want to encourage you and that God loves you. Continue to live for Him and trust Him. Allow Him to build character and patience within you. The sky is the limit for what God can and will do in your life. God may not come when you want Him to but He is ALWAYS on time. He never fails!

- Galatians 6:9
- Isaiah 40:31
- 1 Peter 5:6
- Matthew 21:21-22

God helps us to endure difficult seasons.

THE HOLDER

One night in 2019, I was watching the University of Alabama vs. Duke University football game. I noticed something intriguing as Alabama was kicking an extra point. Tua Tagovailoa, who was the starting quarterback for Alabama, was holding the football for the field goal kicker to kick. The holder (for those who don't watch football) is the player who receives the snap from the long snapper during field goal or extra point attempts made by the placekicker. Typically, the backup quarterback or the punter is the one who holds the ball for field goal and/or extra point attempts.

When I saw that Tua was holding for the kick, I was surprised initially but as I continued to watch, there was one thing that truly impressed me. It was the humility and selflessness that Tua exhibited by being a holder for extra points and field goal kicks. Tagovailoa was a Heisman candidate in 2018 and some say that he could have led the Crimson Tide to a championship. The fact that he held kicks spoke volumes to me because he was humble and selfless enough to do whatever it took to help the team win. He could have easily carried himself in an arrogant manner thinking that he was better than the team because he was the star quarterback but he didn't.

In what ways are you being selfless? Are you being humble with the abilities and blessings that God has given you?

Always remember that apart from God, we are nothing. We are unable to do anything without Him in our lives. We should never forget that. There are times in our lives when we experience success and begin to "feel" ourselves a little bit. One thing that we must realize is that when we are arrogant, we forget about *"where our help comes from, our help comes from The Lord"* (Psalm 121:1-2). As a result of our arrogance, we put ourselves in a position where God will have to humble us. God doesn't humble us to hurt us or because He doesn't want to see us blessed as His children, but He wants to build character within us. God can only use a person with a humble heart to fulfill His kingdom purpose.

Some may wonder, "What are some practical ways to help me remain humble when good things come my way?"

1. Ask God for help in that area and He will help you.
2. Read and memorize scripture as it pertains to humility. Meditate on it and when you sense some arrogance rise up, talk to the enemy and say scripture out loud.
3. Surround yourself with godly people who will not only tell you the truth but will also encourage and support you, keeping you grounded.

Save yourself the trouble of thinking that you can live this life without God because you can't—none of us can. Simply walk with humility in your everyday life and watch what God will do in your life.

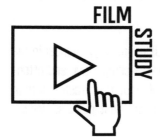

- Philippians 2:3-4
- 1 Corinthians 10:24
- 1 Corinthians 13:4-5
- John 15:5

In what ways are you selfless?

THREE-POINT GAME WINNER

The Portland Trail Blazers played the Oklahoma City Thunder in the first round of the 2019 playoffs. It was a competitive and often-times chippy series with a substantial amount of trash talk from both teams, specifically between each team's best players, Damian Lillard and Russell Westbrook. The best moment of the series was the fourth quarter of Game 5. With the game tied 115-115, Lillard, of the Trail Blazers had the ball with Paul George defending him and hit a DEEP three point shot to not only win the game but also to win the series. The Portland Trail Blazers won the series, 4-1. Lillard ended the game with 50 points.

Despite the trash talk, Portland did a great job of mostly allowing their game to do the talking and they got the last laugh.

Have you ever played a competitive sport?

Have you ever been in a situation where you have been mocked, bullied, or picked on because you were different (whether physically, mentally, a different socioeconomic background, etc.)?

Have you ever been in a situation where you have been hated on for no apparent reason?

Please remember that God loves you very much! God created you in His image (Genesis 1:27) and you are *"fearfully and wonderfully made"*

(Psalm 139:14). You don't have to compare yourself to anyone else (Galatians 6:4-5).

One thing that we must realize is that people were created differently and they have different personalities. Because of this difference, there are different emotions that comes with those personalities. Since people are different, we must understand that we can't control how they act or how they treat us. We can only control how we react and how we treat others.

When people come against you, you don't have to fight your own battles by retaliating. Don't do evil for evil and allow God to do the fighting for you (see Romans 12:17, 19). Oftentimes, the enemy uses people to come against you because He sees you as a threat to him. In addition, the enemy will use your weakness against you. Always remember that his goal is *"to steal, kill, and destroy"* as many people as possible (John 10:10, 1 Peter 5:7).

One thing that we must realize is that Christians will face persecution and *"We wrestle not against flesh and blood (human beings), but against principalities, against powers, against the rulers of the darkness of this world, against spiritual wickedness in high places"* (Ephesians 6:12 KJV).

When you are facing difficult situations with others in which you want to take action and do things your way, don't. Allow God to take control of every situation in your life. When you avoid retaliating and you allow God to fight your battles, you will win every time! Your enemies or people who the enemy uses to come against you will see that light of Jesus Christ shining through you. As a result of Christ's light shining through you, your enemies will have no other choice but to show you love. Who knows? Those same people may eventually ask you about God and want to know more about Him. BOOM! That's the perfect opportunity to witness and preach the Gospel to them. Allow the light of Jesus Christ to shine in your life so that God can ultimately be glorified.

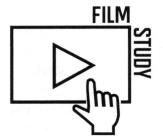

- Deuteronomy 28:9-13
- Matthew 20:16
- Psalms 23:5
- Psalms 110:1-2
- Hebrews 1:13

God can and will fight your battles.

MAKE SOME NOISE!

Sports are great to watch and play. There are many people who are huge sports fans including myself. At sports-themed restaurants, stadiums, and even at home, we cheer for our favorite teams. We cheer when the players do well and yell when our favorite teams don't do so well.

But when we go to church, we find ourselves being quiet and not very enthusiastic about praising and worshipping God—or even going to church in general. We really need to look ourselves in the mirror and see where our heart and priorities are.

Our celebration and praise for our favorite teams (which are composed of other human beings) should never be greater than our praise and worship for our Lord and Savior Jesus Christ, who died for our sins and blesses us with life. We should never find ourselves planning our Sundays—or any other day for that matter—around any sports. Always make God your #1 priority and serve only Him (Luke 4:8).

We don't have to play it cool and act as if we have too much swag to give God the praise because He deserves our praise and worship. If we can be on time for games, work, concerts, and everywhere else, we can be on time for church!

- Matthew 6:21
- Luke 4:8
- Psalm 100:1-5

What God does is worth celebrating!

THE MIRACLE

In 2016, Damari Hendrix was shot in the head in Chicago where he played high school basketball at Foreman High School. He suffered a traumatic brain injury. Damari was given a one percent chance to live. BUT GOD! He healed him and 14 months later, Damari was back on the court.

Damari could easily have given up when he received the doctor's report, but he persevered and didn't allow the negativity to affect him. God is really good! You may have dealt with a life-altering injury or sickness, or you may know someone who has dealt with a negative doctor's report. But through those circumstances, know that God doesn't hate you. He loves you and because He loves you, He can also heal you. God allowed His own son, Jesus, to die for our sins. Jesus not only died for our sins, but He came to save souls so that they can ultimately believe in Him as their Lord and Savior. One more thing that we must remember is that Jesus healed many during His life on Earth. Some examples include:

- Jesus healed the blind and deaf man (Mark 7:31-37).
- Jesus healed Peter's mother in law who was sick with a fever (Matthew 8:14-17).
- Jesus healed someone with a deformed hand (Mark 3:3-5).

- Jesus healed the woman with the issue of blood (Matthew 9:20-22).
- Jesus even raised a young lady from the dead (Matthew 9:18-26).

I do not know about your specific circumstance. However, I do know that everything happens for a reason. So never stop praying, never stop seeking and drawing close to God, and never lose hope. Center yourself around God-fearing, saved people who have your best interest at heart and will pray for you, not condemn you. Finally, put ALL your trust in God.

Remember that God is a healer and no matter what you may be dealing with and how things may look in people's eyes, God is in control and will always make a way out of no way if you put your trust in Him!

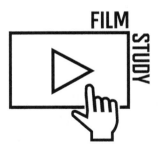

FILM STUDY

- Isaiah 53:5
- Hebrews 11:6
- Mark 11:23-24

God is a healer and can do the impossible!

MANY POSITIONS, ONE TEAM

Within a team—especially in sports like football, basketball, soccer, or baseball—there are many teams compiled of players who play various positions.

For example, there are many positions within the game of football: quarterback, running back, wide receiver, tight end, fullback and the offensive line. These are on the offensive side of the football. Positions on the defensive end of the football include the defensive tackle, defensive end, linebackers, cornerbacks, and safety. Then, there are "special teams" which is comprised of punters, long snappers, holders, field goal kickers, and the coverage team. In addition to those positions, there is a head coach with coaches for most of those specialized positions listed.

In addition, there is the front office or day-to-day staff members who put it all together, the owner/owners, president, director of football operations, general manager, trainers, nutritionists/cooks, security, scouts, and many others.

Someone may say, "Wow, there are a lot of positions within the game of football." They would be correct! There are many positions but each position on the team/organization is very essential for the TEAM to win football games. This is important not only on the field but also off the field as it pertains to volunteering and working within the community.

Like a sports team, the church body is compiled of many positions. For example, the pastor, elders, deacons, evangelists, ushers, youth pastor, overseer, the congregation, etc. Just like any other job, church, or organization, there will be setbacks and difficulties. It is so important that the individuals within must come together to reach that one common goal of fulfilling God's purpose of saving souls—being an ambassador of Jesus Christ to the world while making disciples. Nothing should deter that.

No matter the position, race, denomination, title or how money is in your bank account, all believers, (children of God) are one in the body of Christ. We must stop being divisive, come together and make Jesus known to all the world as we grow in our relationship with God.

FILM STUDY

- Romans 12:4-8
- Galatians 3:28

Every person on the team matters.

TAKING A STAND FOR RIGHTEOUSNESS

J aelene Hinkle played collegiate soccer for the Texas Tech Red Raiders from 2011 to 2014. Then, she was selected seventh in the 2015 National Women's Soccer League College Draft to the Western New York Flash.

In 2017, Jaelene, a believer of Jesus, was invited to play for the USA Women's Soccer team in two international friendlies' games. Days before the games, it was announced that the team's jersey was going to honor the LGBTQ community for Pride Month. As a result, Hinkle thought it was best for her to pray and truly seek God about whether she should wear a jersey that honored the LGBTQ community. She stated in an interview with The 700 Club that "I felt so convicted in my spirit that it wasn't my job to wear this jersey." After seeking God, she withdrew from the games, receiving heavy criticism for her decision.

I commend her for standing up for what is right according to the word of God. Also, I commend her for being willing to listen to the Holy Spirit's prompting, even if following her dream was at stake. This world is full of darkness where sin like homosexuality, abortion, greed, marital infidelity, and sexual immorality is normalized. It is important for Christians to understand that we are meant to be the light of the world and we are called to be different (Matthew 5:14-16 and Romans 12:2).

How do we know the difference between right and wrong or what is a sin or what isn't? We learn this through reading and studying the word of God, the Bible.

The word of God must be the source and guide of our lives. We must study it because it helps us to understand how to be more and more like Jesus Christ and how we should handle every aspect of our daily lives. God is there for us but we must be willing to listen and obey. Remember that He speaks in a small, still voice.

As followers of Jesus, we will have to make decisions that unbelievers will not agree with. We must stand for what is right according to the Bible without compromising our beliefs or worrying about what unbelievers may say or do. It is so important for us to speak the truth in love. Our lives should be Christ-like as we witness and tell others about Jesus Christ. If we do and/or say something that differs from what culture says because of our Christian beliefs (based on the word of God), we should expect to be persecuted by others. We should expect to be persecuted by unbelievers because we are followers of Jesus (2 Timothy 3:12). When we are persecuted, be strong in the Lord and in your beliefs and never waiver from them. The enemy wants to use the world to try deceive us as Christians, causing us to compromise and be like the world.

Be like Christ, not the world. Be bold for the Lord. Be happy when you are persecuted even when it seems like you are being persecuted for no reason. It shows that you are a follower of Christ and you are doing something by the grace of God.

Fear God, not man (Matthew 10:26-28)! One thing that you should ask yourself.are you willing to be obedient to God when He speaks to you no matter the cost?

FILM STUDY

- 1 Corinthians 6:9-10
- 2 Timothy 3:12
- Galatians 1:10
- Romans 12:1-2
- John 8:31-32
- 1 Samuel 15:22
- Matthew 5:12-13
- Leviticus 18:22
- Romans 1:18-32

God's word is our guide.

LET'S·GO!
Week 32

BE THE LIGHT

One night, I watched a postgame interview with Damian Lillard after a big performance with 48 points, 9 rebounds, and 10 assists against the Los Angeles Lakers, resulting in a big win for the Portland Trail Blazers. A reporter asked, "Dame, you mentioned working on your faith.how has that helped you?" Lillard answered, "When Anthony Tolliver [a former teammate who is a Christian] came to the team, he really wasn't pushing [Christianity] but seeing how serious he was about [his faith] and he was constantly offering it out, a Bible study here. CJ [McCollum, a fellow teammate] was like 'Let's go to chapel.'. I also wanted to challenge myself coming into the season to make it to every chapel for every game. And since I've been doing that, I've been able to get deeper into my faith even outside of chapel, getting back to church and be in that environment; just being able to address myself personally and look in the mirror. I think when you do that, you are able to have a lot clearer mind and I think that has been a big help for me."

Leading up to the Lakers game, Lillard—particularly in the six games prior—had been on fire scoring the basketball while getting his teammates involved with assists.

In 2019:

- vs. Dallas Mavericks- 34 points, 10 assists
- vs. Oklahoma City Thunder- 34 points, 6 assists
- vs. Golden State Warriors- 61 points, 7 assists
- vs. Dallas Mavericks- 47 points, 8 assists
- vs. Indiana Pacers- 50 points, 13 assists
- vs. Houston Rockets- 36 points, 10 rebounds, 11 assists (his first career triple-double)

I don't believe it was a coincidence that he was able to play at such a high level during that short period of time.

There were three things that come to mind after watching Damian Lillard's postgame interview.

1. Lillard mentioned that as he was growing in his faith, he had to look himself in the mirror. It is so important for us humble ourselves and recognize that we need God to help and guide us in every aspect of our lives. We must remember that we are nothing without Him. Also, it is so imperative that we take time each day to not only draw close to God through prayer and His word, but also to self-reflect.

2. When we surrender to God and draw close to Him, He gives us peace that most people will not understand (Philippians 4:7). We will begin to grow spiritually, and as a result of our relationship with God, we will begin to see doors of opportunity open (or close) for our benefit (Romans 8:28).

3. The most important thing was seeing how his former teammate, Anthony Tolliver, was able to allow the light of Jesus Christ shine through him (Matthew 5:16) while making a positive impact on Lillard by the way he lived. He was courageous enough to invite him to certain functions like Bible study.

Because of the way Tolliver lived, Lillard was able to see how God was working in his life. He was also able to see an example of a Christian. As a result, Lillard wanted to feel God's presence in his life and desired a relationship with God.

What we say and how we live is pivotal because people are always watching. We may be the only Bible and church that people may see. We must treat everyone like a soul. Love on them, pray with and for them, tell them what God places on your heart and sow that seed. Live holy and right so people can get saved and draw close to God, bringing God the glory.

We all have gifts from God. We all have platforms that God has given us and we are to use those gifts and platforms to bring glory to the name of Jesus, drawing souls to Him. God may not save someone the first time you share the gospel with them. But God can soften that person's heart so that they can eventually invite Him into their lives. Just like plants, the more seeds that are sown into a person's life, there is more of an opportunity for a person to believe in Jesus Christ as his or her Lord and Savior.

What are your God-given gifts?

What are your platforms?

Are you allowing God to use your gifts and platforms to make Jesus' name known?

Don't you know that what you say or do can positively or negatively affect someone's life?

You don't have to worry about what people think about you. Always be bold and courageous while allowing the light of Jesus Christ to shine through you. Not only witness, but also let your life do the talking and watch how God can use you.

- Matthew 5:13
- Matthew 5:16
- 1 Timothy 4:12
- Mark 16:15
- 2 Corinthians 5:20-21

Be the salt and light of Jesus Christ.

33,643 career points. 2007-2008 NBA MVP. 5-time NBA champion. 2-time Finals MVP. 2-time USA Gold Medalist. 1997 Slam Dunk champion. 18-time All Star. 4-time All-Star MVP. 2-time scoring champion (81 points in a game and 60 or more points six times). He even scored 60 points in the last game he ever played! It's safe to say that God gave Kobe Bryant the ability to play the game of basketball.

He had the determination, drive, work ethic, passion, and desire to be great. He strived for excellence every day in his preparation by working out at 5 a.m. and eating healthy. He humbled himself to recognize that he wasn't the perfect basketball player (by the way, no one's perfect) and he began to work hard in practices, games, and even in workouts when others wouldn't. In addition, he would work on the strong and weak points of his game, adding something new every season. He would watch film of himself, his peers, or the players that came before him, and he would ask those same players for advice to help him become the best basketball player he could be.

Bryant once spoke to the University of Alabama football team saying, "If I'm playing against a weaker opponent and I start coasting, I'm doing nothing but building bad habits myself. If you want to play at an excellent level, if you want to do something excellent, you have to be excellent all the time. It's a way of life. When excellence become a habit, that becomes who you are."

Every day in this journey called "life," we will face trials and tribulations, success and testimonies; but what we are doing to overcome them? How can we avoid resting on our laurels while striving for excellence?

We all understand that no one is perfect. The bible says, *"All have sinned and come short of the glory of God"* (Romans 3:23). All we have to do is repent. Because of God's grace, He allowed His son, Jesus, to die for us. One thing that we must do as Christians is strive to be perfected by the Holy Spirit daily. How can we do this?

1. If you are not saved, repent of your sins and totally surrender your life to Jesus Christ. Allow Him to be the Lord of your life.
2. *"Love the LORD your God with all your heart, all your soul, all your strength, and all your mind.' And, 'Love your neighbor as yourself'"* (Luke 10:27). If you love God with all your heart, you will desire to please God. As a result of your love for God, it will translate into loving others.
3. Have a strong desire to stop doing what you used to do and desire to what God wants you to do. Ask God for help and He will help you. John 14:13 tells us that, *"You can ask for anything in my name, and I will do it, so that the Son can bring glory to the Father."*
4. Commit to growing in your relationship with God each day through prayer (communication between you and God) and by reading/studying the bible. Reading and studying God's word will not only provide you with Biblical instructions on how to live as a Christian but it will also help you to grow to be more like Jesus. This is our ultimate goal as Christians.
5. Allow the Holy Spirit, who lives in us upon salvation, to lead and guide you as you go throughout the day. Understand how important it is for you to "be sober and vigilant." In other words, having a

clear mind, being alert to hear God's voice so that you will *"not be ignorant to the enemy's devices"* (2 Corinthians 2:11).

6. As a result of your relationship with God, the Holy Spirit will begin producing the fruits of the Spirit in you. They are love, joy, peace, patience, kindness, goodness, faithfulness, gentleness, and self-control (Galatians 5:22-23).

Life is a journey. We may go through ups and downs but God is there for us. God doesn't want us to perish but have everlasting life. We can't allow the things that are going on in this world to affect how we think and live. We have to think "kingdom over culture." The awesome thing about God is that "He will never leave us nor forsake us" (Deuteronomy 31:8). We may slip up, but we must repent and live the life that God has called us to live.

Always remember that God wants to prune us, shape us, and mold us so that we can be more like Him. The things that we go through in life help us to grow in our faith. Enjoy this wonderful life that God has given you. Grow in your walk with Jesus. Make His name known to people all over the world so that they can know Him also. Find an awesome church with a pastor who preaches the truth in love and doesn't look to preach what you want to hear. And find people who want to experience life together in Christian community in small groups.

Every day, we should always to look to grow as individuals and be the people that God has created us to be. Recognize your need for Jesus to be the Lord and Savior of our life. Center yourself around godly people who have your best interest at heart (you are who you hang around). Stay focused on growing in your relationship with God. In addition, it is so important for us to enjoy the process of life as we grow as Christians. No matter the ups and downs we face, we are not alone with God on our side.

In an interview with Coach Saban of the University of Alabama, Kobe Bryant said, "It seems like this generation is really concerned with the end result of things versus the understanding/appreciating the journey to get there which is the most important thing. There are going to be trials and tribulations that are going to come along with it. You have successes; you have failures but it is all a part of the end game. What I see from a lot of players is that they'll try, they'll push and then all of the sudden they get hit with some adversity and they say 'Nah, let me do something else' instead of staying with it. Just stay with it. A lot of guys just give up on it because it's not happening now." We must realize that regardless of our situation *all things work together for our good"* as the Body of Christ (Romans 8:28). As Christians, we are promised that we will face difficulty and persecution (2 Timothy 2:12, 2 Timothy 3:12) and we can't allow those tough circumstances to cause us to give up on God, and throw in the towel. Persecution and the struggles of life helps us to build character and strength. They also help our faith to grow. James 1:2-3 says, *"My brethren, count it all joy when ye fall into divers temptations; Knowing this, that the trying of your faith worketh patience."*

The end result for all Christians must be going to heaven and witnessing to others so that they can know Jesus Christ and do the same. Always remember that there are no shortcuts to heaven. We are saved by grace not works. Therefore, we must love God. As a result of our love for God, our works will follow. Enjoy the process, enjoy your walk and relationship with God and strive for excellence daily!

- Matthew 6:33
- Philippians 3:12-14
- Galatians 6:9
- Ephesians 4:22-24
- Romans 8:8
- John 14:26
- Colossians 3:17, 23-24
- 1 Corinthians 9:24-27

Each day brings an opportunity to grow.

KINGDOM OVER CULTURE

LET'S·GO!
20 21
Week 34

Many professional athletes grew up dreaming of playing their respective sports at the collegiate and/or professional level. This may be for various reasons including:

- For the love of the game
- They watched their favorite athletes growing up, causing them to want to play the sport.
- They want to better themselves and their lives, and escape from negative family situations or neighborhoods where they grew up.
- They want to provide financial assistance for their families.
- They desire fame, fortune, a lavish lifestyle, and they want to create their own brand.

Some of these athletes may have grown up in Christian households, where faith was most important. They make it to the collegiate and/or professional leagues initially showing that they are Christians. Good fruit is being shown on and off the court, and they even give God the glory in postgame interviews and award shows. But the longer they are in the pros exposed to fame, fortune, premarital sex, drugs, alcohol, etc., the more they allow the enemy through these forms to entice them to be like the world. They begin to use foul language, get tatted up, and becoming more sexually active which translates to having children outside of marriage. They become more and more arrogant thinking that because they have success, they are bigger and better than what they are. As a result, sometimes they hit rock bottom in their careers or in life.

Now, this isn't always the case. There are plenty of strong believers who have used self-control, constantly growing in the Christian faith, and telling others about Jesus. I'm not looking to judge but I am expressing to everyone what can happen when we don't look to grow in our relationship with Jesus, be strong in the faith, center ourselves around godly people, and don't put on the whole armor of God.

It is so important for us to not allow the world or culture to shape how we should live. Instead, we should ALWAYS allow God to be foundation of our lives and allow Him to shape our minds through His Word by reading and studying it daily.

You may believe that living by rules isn't cool. One thing that we must realize is that being a Christian is cool. Just because we are Christians doesn't mean that we can't go to the movies, go bowling, travel, go to sporting events, etc. God desires us to live a great, enjoyable life but He also want us to live life His way according to His word. John 10:10 says, *"The thief does not come except to steal, and to kill, and to destroy. I have come that they may have life, and that they may have it more abundantly."* We must tell others about the life we live for a cool Heavenly Father who loves us unconditionally. God cares for our well-being and He desires us to live according to a Christian standard. Is there any harm in that? No, our Father wants what is best for us. It is cool to grow in our Christian walk. It is cool to have someone who loves you and has your back when it seems like all is lost and there is no hope. It is cool to live for someone who has given the ultimate sacrifice by allowing His own Son, Jesus, to die for our sins so that we wouldn't have to. It is cool to have a Father who, unlike mere humans, forgives us even when we don't deserve it. Do you know what's even cooler? Going to heaven which should be our ultimate goal.

Every day, the enemy is like a thief, looking to steal, kill, and destroy. He is looking to take your peace, your hope, your belief in Jesus Christ, your favor, your prayer, your praise, your love for God and others, your life, and your focus on God and purpose. Our relationship with God must be the number one priority in our lives. As we grow in God, we will grow to be like Jesus daily and we will be able recognize the enemy's schemes. Always counteract evil with good. When the enemy approaches you with negativity, do the opposite so that God can get the glory out of your life.

In Matthew 13:1-23, Jesus gives the Parable of the Farmer Scattering Seed. I love Jesus' parables, by the way! In this parable, a farmer plants seeds (the word of God/gospel message) in four different ways. The four different ways help us understand the ways people respond to the gospel. One of the ways that I want to talk about is where the seed fell on thorns. This represents those individuals who hear the message but all too quickly allow the worries of this life and/or the pleasures of this world to overshadow their desire for Jesus Christ. Therefore, they desire money, fame, women/men, culture, job position, etc. but don't desire to be saved and surrender their lives to God. Ultimately, their hearts begin to harden. We don't want that.

Let's be like those individuals who allow the seed (God's Word) to fall into fertile soil (our hearts) and produce more than what was planted. Every day, let's strive to be people of God who allow the seed to be planted in fertile soil. In other words, we must take in the message of Jesus Christ in our hearts, apply it, and allow it to shape and mold us so that we can produce godly fruit to be more and more like Jesus Christ.

Can we truly say that we have a Kingdom over culture mindset? Are we looking to help others know more about Jesus? Do we want to be like Jesus by growing in our relationship with Him? Make "yes" your answer! Allow the Holy Spirit to help you to win over the temptation that the enemy tries to present in life.

- Matthew 6:33
- 1 Corinthians 9:24-27
- Psalms 1:1-3
- Romans 12:2
- John 15:5
- James 4:6
- 1 Timothy 4:12
- Ephesians 6:10
- 2 Corinthians 2:11
- Matthew 13:1-23

Kingdom > Culture

GOD'S UNEXPLAINABLE PEACE

Trent Dilfer was the sixth overall pick in the 1994 NFL Draft to the Tampa Bay Buccaneers. He played college football at Fresno State University. Dilfer played 14 years as a NFL quarterback. The one-time pro bowler played for various teams such as the Tampa Bay Buccaneers, Seattle Seahawks, Cleveland Browns and San Francisco 49ers. Most notably, he is known for winning the Super Bowl as the starting quarterback with the Baltimore Ravens in 2000. After Dilfer's retirement in 2008, he began working for ESPN as an NFL analyst until 2017. Currently, he is the Head Football Coach for Lipscomb Academy in Tennessee.

In 2003, Dilfer faced what would arguably be one of the most difficult occurrences of his life. He and his family were on a summer vacation at Disneyland where his 5-year-old son, Trevin got a cold. Under normal circumstances, this wouldn't be much of a concern. But in this situation, Trevin's cold did not pass. He began to have a lack of energy and his skin color began to change. Dilfer and his family took him to the emergency room later to find out that his heart was failing. Trevin would require a heart/lung bypass. Thankfully, there was one nurse who was able to keep Trevin's heart pumping enough to put a heart-lung bypass machine on him. Trevin needed to be cared for at Stanford's Children's Hospital which was 2 1/2 hours away and there was no way for the previous hospital to transport him. Through God's protection and grace, a friend of Trent's was able to drive them 200 miles to Stanford. While at the Children's Hospital, Trevin was on the heart-lung bypass machine for 40 days, but he grew weaker and was eventually taken off of life support. On April 27, 2003, Trevin Dilfer passed away.

After Trevin's death, Trent Dilfer experienced peace that others couldn't understand. Most people would be overtaken with sadness after the death of a child. But that is who God is and that is what He does, even in your toughest moments of life. Only He can comfort you with His peace.

When you are going through unimaginably difficult circumstances, the best answer is to draw close to God. When you pray and read the word of God, He will speak to you and provide clarity on the questions that you may have. Be prepared and open your heart to what God has to say to you. It may not be what you want to hear, but it's always important and what you need. In addition, it is important to be quiet after speaking to God so that you can hear His response. Always remember that God speaks in a quiet, still voice. Only then, is He able to take the anxiety away and give you an unexplainable peace through The Holy Spirit that is unexplainable. Those who don't believe in Jesus (and some who claim to be Christians) won't understand the peace that God has given you. They will wonder, "How are you walking around like nothing happened; like you didn't lose a loved one? Or "How are walking around like you didn't lose a job or like your boyfriend or girlfriend didn't break up with you?" There are also people who may know the situation that you are facing and will admire you for how you handle it. Always remember to allow the light of Jesus Christ to shine through you for others to know Him. Draw close to God in prayer and through the Bible not only during the trying times but daily. These things will help you to endure and overcome whatever trial or tribulation you face.

It is also important during those trying times of loss to avoid toxic people. This only brings about negativity. As a result, if you are not spiritually strong, you will begin to be negative and increasingly live in ways that don't honor God. Always remember that you are who you hang around.

Jesus is the Prince of Peace who gives peace of mind and heart that no human or situation can offer. Seek Him, lean on Him, trust Him, and watch what He can do in your life. You may feel down and you may be crying, but it won't last always. Like Psalms 30:5 says, *"Joy will come in the morning."*

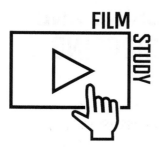

FILM STUDY

- Psalms 34:18
- Philippians 4:6-7
- 1 Peter 5:7
- Matthew 11:28-29
- John 14:27
- Psalms 30:5

Christ offers peace in every situation.

PICKING AND CHOOSING

enjoy sports debate shows like ESPN First Take and Fox Sports 1's Undisputed. These shows provide great insight on various sports leagues such as the NBA, NCAA, NFL, MLB, boxing, and many more. In addition to the insight that they provide, their hosts bring comedic value! There are hosts who do a phenomenal job of delivering information objectively based on stats and the "eye test" (eye test means what your eyes see). There are also times where they express biased opinions or pick and choose certain points about a player based on if they are fans or not.

In the same way, we find ourselves picking and choosing certain parts of the Bible that we agree with. For example, some may say that the Bible doesn't say anything about tithing (giving 10% of your earnings) in the New Testament compared to the Old Testament. Malachi 3:8-10 NKJV from the Old Testament says, *"Will a man rob God? Yet you have robbed Me! But you say, 'In what way have we robbed You?' In tithes and offerings. You are cursed with a curse, For you have robbed Me, Even this whole nation. Bring all the tithes into the storehouse, That there may be food in My house, And try Me now in this,"* Says the LORD of hosts, *"If I will not open for you the windows of heaven And pour out for you such blessing That there will not be room enough to receive it."* Luke 6:38 (NKJV) in the New Testament says, *"Give, and it will be given to you:*

good measure, pressed down, shaken together, and running over will be put into your bosom. For with the same measure that you use, it will be measured back to you."

There are so many times when people pick and choose what they want to believe. Some people do this so that they can continue to live in the way they please, even if their soul is at stake. It starts with your heart and your motives. You must ask God to change your heart so that your desires align with His. Seek His will for your life, not your own.

No matter if it is the Old Testament or New Testament, we must understand that the Bible was written by various writers, but the words written were inspired by God. In other words, God gave the writers the words to say. Therefore, if we say that we are followers of Jesus Christ and that we love God, we must obey what He says. The Bible is a guide to help us to be more like Jesus Christ. There is a popular acronym for the Bible. B.I.B.L.E—"Biblical Instruction Before Leaving Earth." The Bible is here to prepare for us for Jesus' return because He loves us. It is not a book of rules created to hurt us or harm us. Every day, we must strive to be more and more like Jesus by first being willing to humble ourselves and surrender our lives to God daily.

Five ways that we can strive to be more and more like Jesus:

1. *"Jesus replied, 'You must love the Lord your God with all your heart, all your soul, and all your mind.'"* (Matthew 22:37 NLT)
2. *"Then Jesus said to his disciples, 'If any of you wants to be my follower, you must give up your own way, take up your cross, and follow me."* (Matthew 16:24 NLT)
3. *"But seek first the kingdom of God and His righteousness, and all these things shall be added to you."* (Matthew 6:33 NKJV)
4. Hide and memorize the Word of God in your heart.... *"I have hidden your word in my heart,that I might not sin against you."* (Psalm 119:11 NLT)
5. Allow God to guide your life.... *"Your word is a lamp to my feet And a light to my path."* (Psalm 119:105 NKJV)

We can't pick and choose what we want to believe and obey. It is time for us as the Body of Christ to obey God, He loves us and He knows what is best for us.

"So be careful to obey all the commands I give you. You must not add anything to them or subtract anything from them." (Deuteronomy 12:32)

- 2 Timothy 3:16
- Matthew 4:4
- James 1:22
- Hebrews 11:6
- Psalm 51:10

We can't pick and choose what to obey.

WHO HAS YOUR BLIND SIDE?

Michael Oher was an offensive tackle for the Carolina Panthers, Baltimore Ravens, and the Tennessee Titans. An offensive tackle's job is typically to block defenders from getting to the quarterback and watching their "blind side." Blind side in football terms means the side of the field opposite of the way that the quarterback is facing. For example, the right tackle protects the left-handed quarterback's blind side. In Oher's case, he watches and blocks for right-handed quarterbacks when defenders are coming from behind outside of the quarterback's field of vision.

In life, there will be people who may say that they have your best interests at heart, but deep down they don't. They may say that you can trust them but you can't. We are supposed to trust God first and foremost anyway. Contrarily, there are some phenomenal people that God places in your life whom you can hang out with, speak with, pray with, etc. Those individuals can bring the best out of you by motivating you and being honest with you even when you don't want to hear it because they've got your back. When someone comes into your life, truly use discernment and ask God for clarity. Whether that person was sent by Him or the enemy, God will let you know.

Allow friends to come into your life who truly have your best interests at heart and won't leave you alone every time there is a disagreement or when things are inconvenient for them. If a "friend" gets mad at you and loses communication with you every time they get angry, they may not be your true friend. Friends communicate their issues with honesty and love, even if it is with tough love. Allow friends to come into your life who are like-minded, particularly from a spiritual standpoint. Those friends who are spiritually like-minded will hold you accountable, encourage you, and motivate you according to the word of God. Also, allow friends to come in your life who will keep it REAL with you and have your back. Who has your blind side?

FILM STUDY

- Ecclesiastes 4:9-12
- Proverbs 18:24
- Proverbs 27:6
- Proverbs 27:17
- Hebrews 10:24-25
- Galatians 6:1-3

Friends communicate honestly with love.

MY PLAN
VS.
GOD'S PLAN

A fter graduating from high school, Tanner McGrew dreamed of playing college hoops. He wasn't recruited or invited to walk-on to any college basketball teams either. So he decided to go to pursue a partial trombone scholarship as a music major at Division II West Virginia Wesleyan College. During his freshman year, McGrew played intramural basketball. He expected to do the same during his sophomore year until one day, the Head Coach of Men's Basketball team, Patrick Beilein (son of the former University of Michigan coach, John Beilein), saw him working out at the gym. Beilein approached the 6-foot-8 McGrew wondering if he would like to walk on to the basketball team because they needed an additional player. In addition, Beilein said that McGrew probably wasn't going to play.

Next thing you know, Tanner McGrew became a star for the team. During his junior year, he averaged 16 points and 12.2 rebounds per game. He increased his production as a senior averaging 22.6 points and a Division II leading 12.4 rebounds per game. Before the end of McGrew's senior year, someone had reached out to him about playing professional basketball in Australia. After doing some research and getting married to his sweetheart, he decided to take advantage of the opportunity to play in Australia for the South West Metro Pirates where he averaged 21.4

points and 11.7 rebounds per game and was voted Most Valuable Player.

After playing professionally in Australia, McGrew went on to play in Denmark for SISU Copenhagen (2016-2017), where he averaged 16.7 points and 10.5 rebounds per game. After his stops in Australia and Denmark, McGrew went on to play in France before receiving an opportunity to play in the NBA G League with the Memphis Hustle and the Salt Lake City Stars. On February 19, 2019, he received an honor that many basketball players long for. He earned an opportunity to play basketball for his country. He was named a member of the February 2019 USA Basketball Men's World Cup Qualifying Team.

God has most certainly been blessing his life. His plan was to go to West Virginia Wesleyan on a trombone scholarship but he ended up playing basketball at the highest level, professionally and internationally. It is so important for us to set goals for ourselves and *"write the vision and make it plain"* as the Bible says in Habakkuk 2:2. As important as it is to go to God in prayer and ask Him for the desires of our hearts, we must also pray and ask Him what is His will for our lives. Our desires must align with God's desires for us. Every day of our lives, we should always live to glorify and honor Him. We should ask God about what His will because He has blessed us all with various gifts. We are meant to use those gifts for His glory and make the name of Jesus known to the world.

As we grow in our relationship with God, we must understand that *"God's ways are not our ways and His thoughts are not our thoughts"* (Isaiah 55:8-9). The Christian walk is a faith journey in which we must trust God's plan, timing, and purpose for our lives. God has a plan for our lives and doesn't want us to waste our time doing things, pursuing dreams, occupations, business ventures, or relationships that He didn't desire for us in the first place. Sometimes God doesn't allow things to work out the way we planned because:

1. God has a better opportunity or future spouse for us.
2. We are not ready for it spiritually, mentally, physically, financially,

emotionally, etc. God will not give us something that we desire outside of timing. If He gave us what we desired before we were truly ready for it, we could potentially ruin them because of our lack of maturity.

3. God wants to build character and patience in us so that we can be more like Jesus, which is the ultimate goal for Christians. As we grow to be like Jesus Christ, we can be the best husbands, wives, fathers, mothers, professionals, friends, siblings, and children that we can be.

We must mature enough to the point that we are just as happy for the closed doors as the open doors because we know that God is always working behind the scenes on our behalf. Making our relationship with God our first priority in life, obeying His word (the Bible), trusting Him, His timetable, and His plan are extremely important if we truly want to receive everything that He has for us. God is in control and everything He does is for a reason. He is our Heavenly Father who knows what is best for us. When we follow God's plan, He will begin to work in our hearts and lives, opening doors that you would least expect. Others will begin to wonder the secret of how you succeed. That is a perfect opportunity to share the good news of Jesus Christ with them. As a result, God's name will be glorified. Trust God's plan—not your own plan—and watch what God will do in your life.

- Romans 8:28
- Jeremiah 29:11
- Matthew 6:33
- Proverbs 16:1
- Proverbs 16:9
- Philippians 4:6-7
- Isaiah 55:8-9
- Isaiah 46:10

The Christian walk is a journey of faith.

YOU CAN OVERCOME YOUR PAST

Stephen A. Smith was born in the Bronx, New York and raised in the Hollis section of Queens, New York. After graduating high school and attending the Fashion Institute of Technology, he received a basketball scholarship at Winston-Salem State University, where he graduated in 1991. During his time at Winston-Salem State, he wrote a column for the university newspaper.

Smith's professional print media career started working for companies such as the Winston-Salem Journal, the Greensboro News and Record, and the New York Daily News. Next, Smith worked for 16 years at the Philadelphia Inquirer. He began his career at ESPN in 2003 as an analyst for the network's NBA Shootaround (now named NBA Countdown) pre-game show. Since then, he has had phenomenal opportunities with ESPN and ESPN2, including his own television show entitled, "Quite Frankly." In addition, he hosted his own radio show called, "The Stephen A. Smith Show." He is also a very integral part of one of the best sports debate shows on television today, "ESPN's First Take." Smith has had a success-ful career thus far and still has a long career ahead of him.

Ironically, Smith was held back in the fourth grade because he had a first grade reading level. He was even ridiculed by kids in the neighbor-hood because of it. Smith didn't allow what he went through in the fourth grade to discourage him. I'm sure that he used that as motivation to grow and be the best that he can be and look at him now.

Have you ever encountered a situation in your life where you have been picked on by others because of a physical or learning disability? Have you ever been part of a single-family household that is dealing with financial difficulty and you are wondering how you and your family's needs are going to be met? Have you ever felt sad because of a bad breakup with a girlfriend or boyfriend? Have you ever been bullied or persecuted for no reason? Are you part of a family in which your parent has had an addiction? What kind of setbacks have you faced in your life that has caused you to lose hope?

God loves you so very much despite your setbacks or mistakes. As a follower of Jesus Christ, you are never alone and Jesus has left you with an advocate, the Holy Spirit, who lives inside of you. The Holy Spirit leads and guides us and gives us peace that others will not understand (Philippians 4:7), not only in the most difficult moments but in every area of life. You are more than enough, and you are *"fearfully and wonderfully made"* (Psalm 139:14). You are qualified and God did not make a mistake when He made you.

God created all of us for a reason and He has given us all gifts to use for His glory. Never allow anyone to tell you that you don't have the ability to perform any task, skill, hobby, or career path. We don't have to allow our past struggles, setbacks, or difficulties to stop us from accomplishing great things in our lives. It is so important for us to draw close to God and as the Bible says, *"If we draw close to God, He will draw close to us"* (James 4:8). We can draw close to God by growing in our relationship with Him through prayer and reading/studying His Word. As a result, God can give us the strength to move forward from our past so that we can reach our full potential and receive everything that He has for us. For us to reach our full potential, we must seek God's will for our lives, believe in the abilities that He has given us, trust in Him, work hard, and be patient knowing that God will provide for us.

FILM STUDY

- Isaiah 43:18-19
- Proverbs 3:5-6
- 2 Corinthians 3:5
- 2 Corinthians 12:9-10
- Philippians 3:13-14
- Philippians 4:6-8
- Isaiah 26:3
- Habakkuk 2:2-3

We can reach our full potential with God.

IN SPITE OF

In the 2018-19 season, Paul George had an MVP caliber season as the shooting guard for the Oklahoma City Thunder in which he averaged 28.0 points, 8.2 rebounds, and an NBA-leading 2.2 steals per game. In February 2019, he suffered a shoulder injury which somewhat negatively affected his play in the second half of the season. The summer of the 2019-20 season, George had to undergo two shoulder surgeries. On July 10, 2019, the six-time All Star was traded to the Los Angeles Clippers to play with the newly acquired Kawhi Leonard, who was the 2019 NBA Finals MVP. After receiving the news, Paul George was excited because he was able to move close to his home in Palmdale, California (1 hour away from Los Angeles). In addition, he was happy that his parents would be able to see him play every game.

In the first game of the 2019-2020 season, the Los Angeles Clippers played a nationally televised game against the Los Angeles Lakers who added an NBA All Star, Anthony Davis, to their roster. But the Clippers had to do so without Paul George's services as he was recovering from his shoulder surgeries. At last, George returned to the basketball court and into the starting lineup as a member of the Los Angeles Clippers vs. the New Orleans Pelicans (11/14/19). The Palmdale native had a virtuoso performance for a person who just returned from injury with 33 points and 9 rebounds (10-17 from the field, 3-5 from the three-point line, and 10-10 from the free throw line) in 24 minutes. Two days later, George led the Clippers to a 150-101 win vs. the Atlanta Hawks while scoring 37 points (10-17 from the field, 6-11 from the three-point line, and 11-11 from the free throw line) in 20 minutes of action.

Paul George had a phenomenal two game stretch considering he couldn't play competitive basketball for seven months. Some people were surprised that he was able to play as well as he did so quickly. Although, Paul George's first two games were a surprise to some, I'm sure that he wasn't surprised with his performances because he is confident of his abilities based off of the work that he put in on and off the basketball court.

Has there ever been a time in your life in which others have doubted you? Have you ever been told that you aren't worthy? Have you ever been told that you aren't smart enough to graduate from high school or college? Has anyone ever told that you are ugly? Has anyone ever told that you aren't attractive enough because you may be overweight or have a deformity? Have you ever been told that you are not qualified to possess a particular job because you don't have a Masters or doctoral degree? Have you ever been told that you are too short or not strong enough to play a particular sport at the collegiate or professional level?

Never allow others' opinion of you to be your reality. You are worthy. You are smart enough. "You are fearfully and wonderfully made" according to Psalm 139:14. Ladies, you are beautiful. Fellas, you are handsome. God didn't make a mistake when He created you because He doesn't make mistakes. Just because you are not qualified in some people's eyes doesn't mean that you aren't qualified in the eyes of God. No matter your height or weight, you are more than capable of playing college sports and/or going to play professional sports. Always know that *every good and perfect gift comes from above* according James 1:17. God wouldn't tell you to do something if He didn't give you the ability to do it. Also, God wouldn't have given you a gift if He didn't expect for you to use the gift for His glory. Believe in Jesus Christ, put all of your trust in Him, and work hard. Always know that you can do all things through Jesus Christ because God loves you. Do you know why God loves you? Because He is love (1 John 4:16). You are more than capable of doing anything that you put your mind to according to God's will in spite of what people may say or think about you. As a child of God, you will never lose, you will always win!

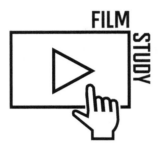

- Romans 8:31
- Deuteronomy 28:13
- 1 John 4:4

You are qualified by God, not people.

GAME SAVING PLAYS

During the 2016 NBA Finals matchup between the Golden State Warriors and the Cleveland Cavaliers, after the Warriors were up 3-1, the Cavaliers bounced back and tied the series, 3-3 behind back-to-back 41-point performances by LeBron James in games 5 and 6 respectively. Game 7 was a classic defensive game like one of those rugged, low scoring games that a person would see in the early 2000's between the Indiana Pacers and the Detroit Pistons. With 1:56 left in the fourth quarter and the game tied 89-89, Andre Iguodala was dribbling the basketball up the court on a fast break. J.R. Smith hustled back to slow him down in time for LeBron James to block Iguodala's shot. Ultimately, Kyrie Irving had the ball in his hands on the right wing and hit a clutch 3 point shot over a Steph Curry contest. The Cleveland Cavaliers went on to win the game and the NBA Finals, 93-89. What a phenomenal clutch play in the closing minutes of the game by LeBron James, hustling back on defense to do his famous "chasedown" to block Andre Iguodala's shot! He could have easily given up on the play because of fatigue but he was willing to do whatever it took to lead his team to victory. In my opinion, one of most clutch shots in NBA Finals' history was Kyrie Irving's three-pointer that put the Cavs up by 3 points in the closing seconds of the game. He could have easily folded under pressure, but he had the confidence to take and make the big shot when it mattered most. Like the quote says, "Big time players make big time plays in big time games." After this win, the Cavaliers made history becoming the first sports team in Cleveland to win a championship (the Cavaliers' first) in 52 years. Also, they were the first team in NBA history to come back after being down 3-1 to win the NBA Finals.

Has there ever been a time where you have felt lost without joy, peace, or hope looking for love but finding it in the wrong places? Maybe you have a family member who passed away, or you were fired from a job, or you were experiencing depression and possibly desiring to commit suicide. Jesus is the answer to all things. He is the cure to all things. He will give you His joy and "a peace that others will not be able to understand" (Philippians 4:7). Have you noticed how there are so many individuals who have all the pleasures of this life like fancy cars, large homes, fame, fortune, investments, sex, etc. but something or someone is missing from their lives? They are lacking happiness, peace, and fulfillment. Jesus can fill the void in our hearts and lives that no one or nothing else can fill.

God sent His one and only Son, Jesus, into this world *"not to judge the world but to save the world through Him"* (John 3:17 NLT). Jesus came into this world to save souls. He also died on the cross as the ultimate sacrifice for our sins so that we wouldn't have to die because of our sins. 2 Corinthians 5:21 says, "For God made Christ, who never sinned, to be the offering for our sin, so that we could be made right with God through Christ" (NLT). Because Jesus Christ died for our sins, we are made right with God; and we are saved by grace.

Two amazing things that stand out about God and the sacrifice that He made were that *"God knew us before we came out of our mother's womb"* (Jeremiah 1:5) and *"while we were yet sinners, Christ died for us"* (Romans 5:8). God knew us before we knew us ourselves. He knows what we need before we need it. God hates sin. It was introduced into the world after Adam and Eve disobeyed God when they ate from the tree of the knowledge of good and evil (Genesis chapters 2 and 3). God wants to save us from our sins. For us to be saved, we must repent of our sins and believe in Jesus Christ. If we repent of our sins and believe in Jesus Christ, we will receive eternal life. Jesus Christ is the only way to God, believe in Him today so that you live for eternity in Heaven.

- Romans 5:8
- Romans 10:9
- John 3:16-17
- Titus 3:5
- Jonah 2:9
- Acts 4:12
- John 14:6

Jesus is the only way to God.

BE LED BY THE HOLY SPIRIT

LET'S·GO!
Week 42

Sports agents play as an integral part in the lives of professional athletes. There are approximately 21,000 agents in the United States. Their duties include negotiating contracts, helping athletes manage their finances, and assisting with handling athletes' legal and business affairs. Some agents can earn a pretty great living depending on the amount of their clients' playing and endorsement contracts. There are many phenomenal agents who truly have their clients' best interest at heart. They provide sound advice and truly care for their clients personally. In addition, they are willing to use flawless negotiating tactics to ensure that their clients' financial needs are met so that their families are taken care of for the rest of their lives.

Although there are many great agents, there are also a few agents who try to entice athletes into being their clients with lies and unfulfilled promises. In life, you will encounter many different individuals from many places, who have different cultures, socioeconomic backgrounds, races, genders with different personalities. Therefore, we must look at others the way that God looks at them while showing love just like Christ did.

Because everyone is different, we must be led by the Holy Spirit and use discernment in understanding who and what is of God. Just like God uses many people to do His will in this world, there are also individuals who are led by Satan. Satan will try use people by attempting to entice them to do things that are not of God and not believe in Jesus Christ as a result. Always remember 1 Peter 5:8, *"Be sober, be vigilant; because your adversary the devil walks about like a roaring lion, seeking whom he may devour."* This is the age of social media where we are exposed to many people with many opinions. Some of those opinions may not align with God's word. There are many false prophets who disguise themselves as true leaders of the faith but are really "ravenous wolves" (Matthew 7:15) who speaks partial truths. It is so important for us to use discernment to understand who is speaking the truth based on the Bible and who is not. What does discernment mean? Discernment is not only knowing the difference between right and wrong. It is knowing the difference between right and almost right.

In order for us to properly understand the difference between right and almost right, we must study the word of God. We must do this not only so that we will know the truth but also so that we can be learn to more like Jesus Christ. 2 Timothy 2:15 informs us to *"Study to show thyself approved unto God, a workman that needeth not to be ashamed, rightly dividing the word of truth."* Once we study the word of God for ourselves, we will be able to distinguish the difference between what is true and false. In addition, we must allow God to touch our hearts and open our eyes and ears to see and hear from God who is truth. Also, we must center ourselves around people who are believers that hear from God. God may be speaking to those individuals to help us to look at things differently than we would have otherwise.

These are the last days and Jesus is coming back soon. If you are not saved, it is time to believe in Jesus Christ and totally surrender your life to God. If you are a believer, focus on God and growing in your relationship with Jesus daily. As we grow in our relationship with Jesus through prayer and studying God's word, we will be able to use discernment. Sometimes, we may miss the mark but we must repent of our sins, learn from our mistakes, and try not to make those same mistakes again.

Don't be ignorant to the enemy's schemes and tactics. You can do that by staying "locked in" on God daily. How can we stay in "locked in?" By keeping the main thing, the main thing. God must take first place in our lives. Focus on growing in your relationship with God and telling others about the good news of Jesus so that they can ultimately know and believe in Jesus Christ.

- Matthew 7:15
- Matthew 24:23-30
- 2 Corinthians 2:11
- 2 Timothy 2:15
- Matthew 28:19-20
- 1 Corinthians 14:33
- John 14:6
- 1 John 4:1
- Luke 20:45-47

Discernment is knowing right from wrong.

SIN SEPARATES

There are many perks that come with becoming a professional athlete. They include:

- Athletic contract
- Endorsements
- Fame
- Generational Wealth
- Fancy cars
- Beautiful home

Those perks, however, don't guarantee happiness or fulfillment. Oftentimes, becoming a rich, professional athlete without Jesus Christ comes with a lot of stress, pressure, and even drama. There are some professional athletes who have received pressure from family members, friends, and acquaintances to give them money. Some of them are pressured by teammates, friends, and even groupies to go drink, abuse drugs, gamble, and party. Some of them deal with marriage issues or if they are single, although they have all the pleasures of life, they feel lonely because they want someone to share those pleasures with. Also, there are many athletes who grew up in Christian households that taught Christian morals and values but as they grew older and excelled in the varsity, collegiate and professional ranks, they began to stray away from God. They allowed distractions that comes with sports like fame, fortune, drug/alcohol/gambling addiction, and/or endorsement/movie/television opportunities to get in the way of their spiritual growth. Those same athletes forget where their abilities come from. As a result, they begin to be arrogant, believing that they can do anything that they want. They forget that "every good and perfect gift comes from above," from God (James 1:17). Always walk in humility or God will humble you.

Another distraction that sometimes come into play as it pertains to sports is the men and women who look to sleep with athletes with an aim to benefit from the athletes' wealth. A lot of times, they fall into the temptation of having premarital sex with one or multiple partners which leads to sexually transmitted diseases, unwanted pregnancies, and/or baby mama or baby daddy drama. In addition, there is cheating involved. Some athletes are married but decide to cheat on their spouses. They expect to receive temporary satisfaction, which ultimately leads to heartache. Some athletes look to enhance their performance in their respective sports by using performance enhancing drugs. This can also lead to trouble.

Please don't get me wrong. There are many Christian professional athletes who have had successful lives and didn't allow the pleasures of life to stunt their spiritual growth. Unfortunately, there seems to be more of the opposite. Like athletes, *"All have all sinned and come short of the glory of God"* (Romans 3:23). Sin was introduced into the world when Adam and Eve ate fruit from the tree of the knowledge of good and evil after God had forbidden Adam not to eat from that tree.

One may ask, "What is sin?" Sin is an immoral act that contradicts the word of God. We must understand that sin separates us from God (Isaiah 59:2) and it could ultimately lead to death (Romans 6:23). If the sinner doesn't repent of the sin committed and believe in the Lord Jesus Christ as his or her Lord and Savior, he or she will live for eternity in hell. We have the power to conquer sin, but it starts with our heart. We must ask that God change the desires in our heart so that our desires will align with God's desires for us. It is so important that we grow in our relationship with God so that we can model our lives after Jesus Christ. In addition, we must use discernment (understanding the difference between right and wrong) when faced with tempting situations and be led by the Holy Spirit.

None of this possible without salvation. God allowed His Son, Jesus Christ, to die for our sins so that we wouldn't have to. Because of Jesus' death on the cross, God offers His grace (unmerited favor). Because we have all sinned, it is critical that we repent of our sins. If you were to die today, where would you be for eternity, Heaven or hell? If you are unaware of that answer, you must repent of your sins, believe in Jesus Christ, and totally surrender to God today. You do not have to be a prisoner to sin.

FILM STUDY

- Titus 2:11-12
- Ephesians 2:8-9
- 2 Corinthians 5:21
- 1 John 1:9
- John 3:16-17
- Romans 10:9
- Romans 8

Sin separates us from God.

THIS JOURNEY CALLED LIFE

Week 44

In a Jacksonville Jaguars press conference after returning to the starting lineup, Quarterback Nick Foles said, "At the end of the day, it's like, 'God, if this is the journey You want me to go on, I'm going to glorify You in every action, good or bad.' I still could have joy in an injury." In 2019, Foles was out of the lineup due to a broken left clavicle that he suffered in week one vs. the Kansas City Chiefs. He could have easily given up or been depressed especially after signing a huge free agent deal with the team the prior offseason. Foles was able to find his peace in Jesus Christ because his identity is in Jesus Christ.

In this journey called "life," we face struggles and difficulty. One thing that we should understand is that although we will be blessed as Christians, there will also be times when we will suffer and face persecution. During the difficult moments of life, we must endure, be patient, and trust God without complaining. Also, as we grow in our relationship with God, He will produce good fruit, one of which is joy through the Holy Spirit (Galatians 5:22-23). Timothy 2:12 reminds us that *"If we suffer, we shall also reign with him: if we deny him, he also will deny us."* In addition, God promised that *"He will never leave us or forsake us"* (Deuteronomy 31:6, Hebrews 13:5) because He loves us.

Through the difficult moments of life whether if it is physical/financial issues, marital issues, emotional pain because of death to a loved one, dealing with depression, etc., you can always find faith, peace, hope, strength, and joy in Jesus Christ. It is so imperative that we draw close to God in prayer and through studying God's word, not only during the difficult moments but in every aspect of life. In addition, put your faith in Jesus and He will help ease your pain. There are many times when God will allow things to occur in our lives so that we draw closer to Him, grow in Him, and so that He build character within us.

Through the ups and downs, we must praise God and be thankful not only for the closed doors/opportunities but also for the open ones. Remember that every opportunity isn't from God. Seek God about His plans for your life and trust His timing. God ALWAYS knows best! Praising God and having faith in Him in those moments opens the door for God to work in your life and helps you grow as a Christian as a result.

FILM STUDY

- Philippians 4:6-7
- James 1:2-4
- James 4:8
- 1 Peter 5:7
- 1 Corinthians 15:58
- Galatians 6:9
- Matthew 11:28
- 1 Peter 5:7

When times are hard, we can endure.

A FIRM FOUNDATION

Philip Rivers is a 6'5", 217-pound quarterback from Decatur, Alabama who played college football at North Carolina State University. He was drafted fourth overall in the 2004 NFL Draft by the New York Giants before being traded to the former San Diego Chargers for the first overall pick of the draft, Eli Manning. Rivers went on to have a successful 16-year career with the Chargers. He was able to accumulate 59,271 passing yards and 397 passing touchdowns during his tenure as a Charger. Also, he was named AP Comeback Player of the Year in 2013. In March 2020, the eight-time Pro Bowler signed with the Indianapolis Colts as a free agent.

While Rivers is a phenomenal quarterback, it is only through God's grace. He once said concerning his marriage, "I think that the center of our marriage and the foundation of our relationship was on Jesus. That is why it's worked to this point. I hope that God has used me to touch one of you in your faith journey with Jesus." Rivers has been married to his wife, Tiffany, since 2001 and they have nine children. What I learned most about Rivers' statement was the importance of allowing God to be the foundation of marriage.

One thing that we must realize is that God loves us so much and because He loves us, He wants a close, intimate relationship with us. As we look to grow in our personal relationship with God as followers of Jesus Christ, we will learn how to be like Christ and ultimately receive eternal life which is the goal for all Christians.

If you are single, you must understand that you cannot expect God to bless you with a man or woman of God if you are not one yourself. Men, it is critical that we learn how to love and lead. First and foremost, God must be the foundation of our lives and we must learn how to love Him with all of our hearts, soul, strength, and mind (Luke 10:27). As a result of our love for God, we will learn to how to love our future wives as Christ loves His bride, the Church (Ephesians 5:25). As we look to grow in our faith walk, the Holy Spirit will bear fruit in our lives so that we can satisfy our spouses' emotional/spiritual needs and lead our wife well with love, joy, peace, goodness, kindness, gentleness, patience, and self-control (Galatians 5:22-23). Ladies, it is important that you learn how to love God, surrender to Him, and allow Him to be the foundation of your life. As a result, you will learn how to love and submit to your future husband. "Submission" can often be a misunderstood word. In marriage, husband and wife must understand the importance of humility and a willingness to serve. Both parties must understand that in order for God to be a solid foundation in your marriage, you must humble yourself enough to recognize that you are not in your marriage alone. When both spouses walk in humility, they are willing to serve one another. Husbands are willing to submit to their wives with love and the wives are willing to submit to their husbands with respect. Fellas, be respectful in your authority over your household.

When God is the foundation of your individual lives, you will be able to bring something to the table when God sends your spouse. Matthew 6:33 informs us to "But seek first the kingdom of God and His righteousness, and all these things shall be added to you." When God is first your life, the desires of your heart comes. Patience, trust in God, and seeking Him first in your life are critical components in order to prepare for your God-given spouse.

If you are married, have quiet time with God individually like Jesus did (Luke 5:16) and pray and study the Word of God together so that you both can grow spiritually. As a result of your spiritual growth as a couple, you will ultimately learn to be with one accord with one another while being phenomenal parents to your children as you teach them biblical principles. When you and your husband or wife's marriage is rooted and grounded in God, you will learn how to communicate in the good and bad times. As the body of Christ, you may face difficulties in marriage at times but know that God is with you and you will overcome any situation.

If you don't allow God to be the foundation of your life individually or in your marriage, you will not be able to be the man or woman that God has called you to be. God is the firm foundation that we need. When He is the firm foundation of our lives, we will not be destroyed or perish. Matthew 7:24-27 says, *"Anyone who listens to my teaching and follows it is wise, like a person who builds a house on solid rock. Though the rain comes in torrents and the floodwaters rise and the winds beat against that house, it won't collapse because it is built on bedrock. But anyone who hears my teaching and doesn't obey it is foolish, like a person who builds a house on sand. When the rains and floods come and the winds beat against that house, it will collapse with a mighty crash."* When God is at the forefront of your marriage, it will begin to bear fruit and you will see great results.

FILM STUDY

- Genesis 2:24
- Ephesians 5:21-33
- Proverbs 31:10-31
- Luke 5:16
- Joshua 24:15
- 1 Corinthians 11:3

God must be the firm foundation for life.

LET'S·GO! Week 46 — THE ADVOCATE

In the game of baseball, catchers communicate with pitchers using a series of nonverbal signals that is sometimes given to them by the manager/coach. The finger signals verbalize the various types of pitches, whether if it is a fastball, knuckleball, curveball, slider, change-up, etc. In addition, the pitcher and catcher go through a series of signals until they agree on a good pitch selection. Typically, the most common way for the catcher to successfully relay a signal is using the fingers of his throwing hand. The pitcher and catcher will not be able to communicate verbally because they would give the pitch type away to the opposite team who is batting or on base. Pitching signals are essential throughout a baseball game especially when the manager, pitcher, and catcher understands the tendencies of the batters on the other team. For baseball players, it takes time and effort to film study your opponent to properly distinguish their preferences. The right pitching signal will not only help the pitcher and catcher to be on the same page, but it will increase the chances of delivering strikeouts and limit walks, which can hopefully lead to wins.

Football has its own secret signals. Perhaps you've noticed how coaches or the offensive coordinators would wear headsets during professional football games. They do this to communicate with their players on the field by calling offensive or defensive plays. In college football (in particular, the NCAA), while coaches and coordinators also wear headsets, you will also see teams verbalize to their players on the field using signals or huge play cards that coordinators or the backup quarterback hold over their heads. These provide signals to call plays, give a formation (determine how players position themselves on the field), speed up the communication between the offensive coaches and players, or fool the defense as a decoy. On these play cards, you will find four pictures of various things. For example, words, movie references, sports teams, memes, etc. One difference that you will find between NCAA football and the National Football League (NFL) is that the NFL quarterbacks have microphones in their helmets. Therefore, they have more leeway to call their own plays and audible (change plays at the line depending on what they see at the line) into another play. Pitching signals, play cards, headsets, and/or any nonverbal signals are key particularly as it pertains to communicating in huge arenas/stadiums with load, raucous fan bases.

Has there ever been in time in your life where you felt alone? Guess what? You don't have to feel alone. The Holy Spirit is available to us and lives inside of the hearts of those who believe in Christ Jesus (1 Corinthians 3:16, John 14:27). The Trinity is one God in three persons; one of whom is the Holy Spirit, who is the third person of the Trinity (the first is God and the second is Jesus Christ). Before ascending into Heaven, Jesus left us an advocate and that is the Holy Spirit (John 14:26) who is able to lead and guide us as we go throughout our daily life. John 16:13 lets us know that *"when the Spirit of truth comes, He will guide you into all truth. He will not speak on His own but will tell you what He has heard."*

Has there ever been a time where you felt sad? God will give you the strength to pray regardless of how you may be feeling or even if you simply don't know what to say in prayer. The Holy Spirit will give us the words to say and He will pray on our behalf as it says in Romans 8:26-27.

Has there ever been a time where someone made you upset to the point where you wanted to yell at them or seek revenge? Always remember that the Lord always has our backs and He will fight our battles. God doesn't want us to retaliate and make a bad decision that we will regret later. That is why it is critical for us to allow the Holy Spirit to bear His fruit within us so that we can love and serve others (Galatians 5:22-23).

Have you encountered a situation where you needed to make a difficult decision (accepting a job, leaving a job, courting a significant other, finding a church home, etc.)? God wants a close relationship with you in which He wants you to consult Him before making any major decision. God doesn't want us to consult Him because He wants to smother us but because He knows "the end from the beginning" (Isaiah 46:10). Also, He wants to save us from ourselves. He wants us to seek His will for our lives because He knows what is best for us. *"God's thoughts are not our thoughts and His ways are not our ways"* (Isaiah 55:8). Sometimes we make monumental mistakes because of our flesh, lack of patience, disobedience, and our unwillingness to keep God at the forefront of our lives. Proverbs 3:5-6 says, *"Trust in the Lord with all your heart, And lean not on your own understanding; In all your ways acknowledge Him, And He shall direct your paths."* Receive clarity from God first in prayer about the decisions of life and He will prompt you through the Holy Spirit as it pertains to the next step to take. We all have all made mistakes in our lives, but God's grace is sufficient enough to forgive us of our sins if we repent.

The Holy Spirit is our "ultimate signal caller" who can help us fully understand the difference between right and wrong. Understanding the difference is so important because there are two destinations that people will live for eternity, either heaven or hell. The awesome thing about God is that He loves us so much that He doesn't want any one of us to perish (2 Peter 3:9). God is like a gentleman who doesn't force us to serve Him. He gives us the free will to make the decision to surrender our lives to Him or reject Him. Although He is a loving God, He is also a just God. We will face the consequences for the decisions that we make. Eternity depends on it. Those who decide to reject God and are unwilling to repent of their sins will live for eternity in hell. But God made the ultimate sacrifice by allowing His Son, Jesus to die for our sins on our behalf. As a result, we can believe in Jesus Christ, repent of our sins, have a relationship with Him, and have eternal life in heaven. The amazing about Jesus Christ is that He is not only the Son of God, but He is also our friend. What a friend we have in Jesus!

Seek God first in your life through communication with Him in prayer, studying the Bible, and being led by the Holy Spirit. Then watch how God will change your life for the better. The Holy Spirit serves so many functions in the lives of Christians. If you are a Christian, are you willing to allow God to take the lead through the Holy Spirit, if you haven't done so already? If you are not a Christian, let's change that and make Jesus Christ the Lord of your life today.

FILM STUDY

- Romans 8:10-20
- Romans 12:19
- 1 John 4:7-21
- Galatians 2:20
- Ephesians 1:13-14

With God, you never need to feel alone.

THE PREPARATION OF THE NEW ENGLAND PATRIOTS

The New England Patriots team has been a dominant NFL franchise for a long time. From 2002-2019, they have won six Super Bowl championships (2002, 2005, 2014, 2015, 2017, 2019) and 11 American Football Conference (AFC) championships. Many people may wonder how they win so many games. They have been able to play with a high level of consistency through phenomenal coaching, great quarterback play, and a no nonsense approach that doesn't tolerate outside distractions. When players arrive to play for the Patriots, they have a full understanding of their roles and know how to do their job well individually so that the team can ultimately succeed.

One thing about the New England Patriots franchise that is different from any other NFL franchise is their preparation. Head Coach Bill Belichick and his coaching staff do a great job of preparing the team for every game. No matter the opponent, no matter the score, no matter if there is rain, sunshine, or snow, primetime television or out of market games, the New England Patriots give their very best every game. They rarely beat themselves. They typically create more turnovers on defense than they commit on offense. The reason is because of their discipline. The Patriots seem to always understand situational football whether it is knowing how to play two minute offense or keeping the ball out of the opponent's possession during crucial points of games. The coaching staff does a phenomenal job of creating great offensive, defensive, and special team schemes that will help put to the team in a great position to win. In addition, the players do a great job of executing the game plan on offense and defense.

In addition to being a phenomenal football team and being coached by the greatest NFL head coach (in my personal opinion), during those seasons they also had Tom Brady, one of the greatest quarterbacks of all time. But the reason that the Patriots have consistently won every year is because they are always prepared to play through great coaching that implements effective schemes. Most importantly, they respect every opponent no matter the opponent's win-loss record.

These are the last days and Jesus is coming back soon. The enemy is looking to tempt as many people as possible through sin ranging from sexual immorality, homosexuality, lies, hatred, rage/anger, greed, etc. The enemy is blinding so many people's eyes in this world and lying to people to the point where they are confused believing that *evil is good and good is evil"* (Isaiah 5:20). It is so important for us as Christians to "not be ignorant to the enemy's devices" and "be sober and vigilant" so that we won't fall into the enemy's trap. What does it mean to "be sober and vigilant?" It means being temperate, careful, and aware. It is important for us as the Body of Christ to be prepared for the return of Jesus. In order for us to prepare for the second coming of Christ, we must draw close to God and grow in our relationship with Him through prayer and studying the Bible. As we grow in our relationship with God, we will learn how to be a Christian which means "Christ-like." Every day, we must live life on purpose for God and recognize that we cannot live life without Him. We should not only grow as follower of Jesus but we must also present the Gospel of Jesus to those who don't know Him. John 3:16-17 reminds us, *"For God so loved the world that He gave His only begotten Son, that whoever believes in Him should not perish but have everlasting life. For God did not send His Son into the world to condemn the world, but that the world through Him might be saved.*" Those who live a life of sin and are unwilling to repent and surrender their lives to God will live for eternity in hell. Those who "confess with their mouth and believe in their heart that Jesus Christ was raised from the dead, they will be saved" (Romans 10:9) and ultimately live for eternity in Heaven. Are you prepared for Jesus Christ's return?

FILM STUDY

- 1 Peter 5:8-9
- 2 Corinthians 2:11
- Ephesians 6:10-11
- John 10:10
- James 4:8
- Isaiah 54:17
- Luke 21:5-36
- Luke 21:34-36

Are you ready for Christ's return?

IT'S NEVER TOO LATE

V ic Fangio has 40 years of coaching experience, having coached in the NFL for 32 of those years. Fangio served as defensive coordinator for 20 of the last 24 seasons at the NFL or college level (Stanford University, San Francisco 49ers, Chicago Bears, Houston Texans, and many more). After 40 years of serving as an assistant coach, he received his first head coaching opportunity with the Denver Broncos.

I went to Liberty University where I received a Bachelor's degree in Sport Management. I wanted to major in Sport Management to coach college basketball, specifically at The University of North Carolina at Chapel Hill. Those who major in Sport Management desire to have a long-term career as a sports agent, working in parks and recreation, working in some capacity for a collegiate or professional sports league, becoming a coach for a sports team, or becoming an athletic director at the middle school, high school, or at the collegiate level. Most people who desire to work in the sports industry could attest that they have to work a considerable number of hours with minimum pay, especially as an entry-level employee. Also, they recognize that they must start from the bottom and move up from there. In other words, they would have to be tenured employees who work hard and excel on their job for them to grow in their respective careers. I would suggest that Vic Fangio had dreams

133

of becoming a NFL Coach. He could have easily given up when opportunities closed, head coaching opportunities arose, or after coaching 40 years of football as an assistant coach or coordinator. Because of this, I truly respect Fangio for his work ethic and unwillingness to give up even when it would have been easy to do so.

Have you ever wondered when your blessing is coming? Always remember *"But they that wait upon the LORD shall renew their strength; they shall mount up with wings as eagles; they shall run, and not be weary; and they shall walk, and not faint"* (Isaiah 40:31 NKJV).

When is God going to answer my prayers? Always remember to *"pray without ceasing"* (1 Thessalonians 5:17 NKJV).

Maybe you have served on your job or church for a substantial period of time and you are wondering when your promotion is coming. Remember God knows about everything that we are facing, and we must *"Count it all joy when you fall into various trials, knowing that the testing of your faith produces patience. But let patience have its perfect work, that you may be perfect and complete, lacking nothing. If any of you lacks wisdom, let him ask of God, who gives to all liberally and without reproach, and it will be given to him. But let him ask in faith, with no doubting, for he who doubts is like a wave of the sea driven and tossed by the wind"* (James 1:2-6 NKJV).

Have you ever been declined a job, fired (for no reason), or laid off and you are wondering why? Romans 8:28 reminds us that *"All things work together for good to those who love God, to those who are the called according to His purpose."*

Are you single and wondering when you are going to be married? Are you a married believer who is married to an unbeliever and you have been praying to God for your spouse to be saved? Have you and your spouse been trying to have a baby? Have you been praying for God to save a friend, family member, or colleague? Never stop praying to God. Maybe God wants to know how patient and faithful you are going to be even when things in life do not go the way that you expect them to do. *"The effective, fervent prayer of a righteous man avails much"* (James 5:16 NKJV). No matter what your desire is, remember that *"There is nothing too hard for God"* (Genesis 18:14).

Maybe you are older and want to return to school. Understand that it isn't too late to earn your degree. Focus on the purpose that God has for your life and remember that purpose doesn't have an expiration date.

Are you being thankful for and faithful over the things that God has been doing in your life? *"He who is faithful in what is least is faithful also in much; and he who is unjust in what is least is unjust also in much"* (Luke 16:10). God has a plan for your life. His plan is *"of good, not of evil, to give you a future and a hope"* (Jeremiah 29:11). Maybe God hasn't elevated you because He knows that you are not ready for it yet. Maybe God wants to make sure that your heart is in the right place. Maybe you haven't received what you asked God for because He wants you to draw close to Him and be more like Him. Maybe you are not doing anything wrong. You probably didn't receive what you asked God for because it wasn't meant for you to have.

God always protects and saves His people from themselves. There is a season for everything and maybe this isn't your season for what you asked God for. Oftentimes, God must prepare us, shape, and prune us. If we receive what we asked God for and it wasn't in His timing, then we could mess things up because we weren't spiritually mature enough to receive it. It is so important for us to understand this because God has a plan for us. We must seek God's will for our lives. He knows what is best for us, why it is best for us, when it is best for us, and how it is best for us. *"For My thoughts are not your thoughts, nor are your ways My ways," says the Lord."* (Isaiah 55:8). When our desires align with God's will for us with patience, focus and total reliance on Him, then we will be able to receive everything in His timing. Trust God's timetable.

FILM STUDY

- Isaiah 55:8-9
- Ecclesiastes 3:1
- Luke 1:37
- Matthew 19:26
- Galatians 6:9
- 1 Corinthians 15:58

There is a season for everything. Just wait!

LET'S·GO!
Week 49

PRISONER OF UNFORGIVENESS

T he Last Dance" was an ESPN documentary that went behind the scenes of the 1997-98 NBA Champion Chicago Bulls. Part of the documentary discussed the rivalry between the Chicago Bulls and the Detroit Pistons in the last 80's and early 90's. It also discussed the Pistons' dominance over the Bulls, particularly during the early years of Michael Jordan's career. The Bulls initially had difficulty defeating the Pistons in the playoffs because of their physicality and an implemented defensive philosophy called "The Jordan Rules." The Detroit Pistons won two straight NBA championships in 1989 and 1990.

With The Jordan Rules, the Pistons focused on a few principles as it pertained to guarding Michael Jordan.

Joe Dumars or Dennis Rodman would guard Jordan man-to-man. With Dumars guarding him, he would force and funnel Jordan to his left side. As he drove to the basket, the Pistons' big men, Bill Laimbeer, Rick Mahorn, and James Edwards, met him at the rim with physicality. They had a mentality of "no easy baskets."

Also, the Pistons double teamed Jordan with the focus of making him pass the ball to his teammates instead of him playing one-on-one. Their goal was to make his teammates beat them because Jordan was that much of a scoring threat on the basketball court.

In the 1991 Eastern Conference Finals, the Chicago Bulls finally over-came the Detroit Pistons as they swept them 4-0. One memorable mo-ment of that series was when the Pistons walked past the Bulls' bench before the final clock expired without shaking one member of the Bulls' hands. That moment displeased Michael Jordan and his Bulls' team-mates. The Pistons' bad sportsmanship stuck with Jordan for a very long time. Twenty-nine years later, during the Last Dance documentary (2020), Jordan said that he hated Isiah Thomas, who was the star of the Detroit "Bad Boys" Pistons. M.J. stated, "I respect Isiah Thomas' talent. To me, the best point guard of all time is Magic Johnson and right behind him is Isiah Thomas. No matter how much I hate him, I respect him." One may wonder why Jordan hated Thomas so much. Although Jordan had respect for Thomas' game, this hatred was an example of unforgiveness and a grudge that Jordan was harboring in his heart.

I was watching a clip from the Fox Sports 1 sports debating show, "Un-disputed" where Shannon Sharpe and Skip Bayless discussed Michael Jordan's comments about Isiah Thomas. Shannon Sharpe had one of the most powerful quotes. Sharpe stated that his grandmother said this to him as a little boy, "There can never be freedom without forgiveness. I think people look at freedom as being incarcerated—my inability to go somewhere, to do something, freedom of speech, freedom of expression, freedom of assembly—but no. Your emotions, your feelings can be held hostage and can be in bondage and you will never be free." This inspira-tional statement from Shannon Sharpe helps us to recognize the impor-tance of forgiveness.

Has anyone broken your heart? Have you ever been mistreated by a friend, family member, coworker, classmate or an enemy of yours? Have you ever been in a toxic relationship or marriage in which the other person cheated on you? Have you ever been physically or sexually assaulted? Have you encountered a situation in which a person who you considered to be a close friend mocked you or talked negatively behind your back? Have you ever grown up without your biological mother and/or father in your life? Have you had a family member or friend who was murdered?

We have all dealt with situations in which we felt mistreated, but it is so important for us to recognize how much God has forgiven us for the sins that we have committed (when we repent). God allowed His Son, Jesus, to die for our sins. As a result, those who repent of their sins and believe in Jesus Christ as their Lord and Savior will be saved. When we believe in Jesus Christ, we are made right with God, and receive His grace, which is His unmerited favor. As believers of Jesus Christ, we have the Holy Spirit who lives inside of us. Every day, we must understand the importance of "loving God with all of our heart, mind, soul, and strength" as it states in Matthew 22:37. When we love God with all of our might, then we will be able to do what the next verse (v. 38) says, "Love our neighbor as ourselves." Daily, we must ask God to help us produce the fruits of the Spirit within us (peace, love, joy, patience, goodness, kindness, faithfulness, gentleness, and self-control) so that as we can grow in our relationship with God and be more like Christ. Loving God and others is so important because it helps us to recognize the grace that God has given us when we sin. Remember that sin separates us from God (Isaiah 59:2), but by God's grace, we are able to repent of our sins and draw close to God. 1 John 1:9 reminds us *"If we confess our sins to Him, He is faithful and just to forgive us our sins and to cleanse us from all unrighteousness."*

Are you having difficulty forgiving the person or people that have mistreated you? Is it because the pain or hurt that they caused was too difficult to overcome? Romans 8:37 informs us that, *"Yet in all these things we are more than conquerors through Him who loved us."* We can overcome our past hurt, pain, trauma with God's help. We must go to God in prayer asking Him to give the peace and the strength to forgive and He will do so. We must desire to have a mind of Christ.

A couple of the major reasons why we have not been able to forgive is because of pride and/or fear that we will be hurt again. When we are unwilling to forgive, we will be trapped as a prisoner of unforgiveness. We must break free from bondage and captivity so that we can be all that God desires us to be and so we can receive everything that He has for us. For us to truly forgive, we must humble ourselves before God humbles us. Once we forgive, we will receive freedom and feel better emotionally and mentally. Your forgiveness can be testimony to the person who hurt you and they can ultimately be saved (if they aren't already).

Never allow a grudge or unforgiveness to hold you captive. Honestly, do we have a right to hold a grudge or be unwilling to forgive especially when God doesn't hold a grudge toward us? No, we do not. I know that the pain, hurt, and trauma is too difficult to move forward from, but I know a God who cares for you and wants to give you peace. 1 Peter 5:7 says that you are to "cast all your care upon Him, for He cares for you." You can move forward and grow in God, but you must seek Him. When "you draw close to Him, He will draw close to you" according to James 4:8. In addition, we must remember to forgive those who we consider to be our enemies. The enemy is looking to distract and destroy as many people as possible. He does this by attacking our minds and tempting us to do wrong. 1 Peter 5:8 reminds us to *"Be sober, be vigilant; because your adversary the devil walks about like a roaring lion, seeking whom he may devour."* When people come against us, we must remember that we are not fighting against mere humans. We are in a fight with the devil himself and he is using people to get to you. When you were in school, you couldn't excel to the next grade until you passed your tests and quizzes. Likewise, the devil will continue to use people to get to you until you pass the tests.

Please remember when you forgive, it is imperative to avoid harboring a perspective of "I'm going to forgive but I'm not going to forget." Is this truly forgiveness? No, it isn't. With God, you can be free.

- Matthew 5:43-45
- Matthew 6:9-15
- Matthew 18:21-22
- Mark 11:23-26
- Luke 6:37
- Ephesians 4:31-32
- Ephesians 6:10-12
- Galatians 5:22-23
- Jonah 4

Don't allow grudges to hold you captive.

LET'S·GO!
Week 50
IT'S IN THE SMALL THINGS

There are many roles on a team that basketball coaches, staff, and players are given. They are necessary in order for the team to function, excel, and reach their ultimate goal of winning. The head coach is the leader on the bench. There are assistant coaches and athletic trainers who prepare their players physically for the game with stretching and taping them in addition to helping those who are injured. Next, you have the players. Their roles can vary. There are star players whose role is to score the basketball. There are team leaders who inspire, encourage, and motivate on and off the court. Then, there are those who practice with the team but may not play a lot during the games. Other roles are to hustle and be a defensive stopper. A defensive stopper is willing to do whatever it takes on the defensive end of the basketball court to help his or her team be successful. This includes blocking shots, stealing the basketball, getting deflections, or even taking charges.

Charges drawn is a very underrated statistic that isn't necessarily flashy, and it may not cause others to watch highlights because of it. However, taking charges is just as effective as getting a steal, blocking a shot, or getting a deflection. When a person takes a charge, the defensive player gets in the way of the offensive player in hopes of getting a defensive stop and ultimately helping his or her team get another offensive possession.

One player who has had tremendous success at taking charges during his 12-year NBA career is the 6'9" forward for the Utah Jazz, Ersan Ilysova. During the 2016-17 season, he led the NBA with 36 charges drawn. The next season, he was second in the league with 32 charges. Also, Ilysova led the NBA with 49 charges during the 2018-19 season. In addition to his amazing feel of the game on the defensive end, Ersan Ilysova has had an amazing career of scoring the basketball with his great shooting touch from the perimeter. The sharpshooting charge taker has a career scoring average of 10.2 points per game.

Have you ever thought about some small things that God has done in your life? For example, being alive for another day, a random person paying for your coffee at a coffee shop, someone letting you in line in front of them at a grocery store because they notice that you have less items to checkout than they do, etc. What if you someone who is less fortunate than you are approaches you and ask for money or help in general. Are you thankful to God for blessing you with the finances to be able to help? Always remember that we are blessed to be a blessing.

In this social media culture, we begin to compare our lives to others, or we compare what we have to what others have. We fail to realize that we are doing nothing but causing ourselves unnecessary stress. God created us all differently. We are of different races, from different cultures, with different socioeconomic backgrounds, personalities, testimonies, etc. God has given us various gifts that we are to use to glorify His name and make Him known to others in this world. It is so important for us to recognize that everyone may be at different points in their walk with God. We don't know what others have gone through to get to where they are. Focus on being the best person that you can be knowing that God has a plan for your life. Grow in your personal relationship with God so that you can be all He has called you to be and so that you can receive everything He has for you. Philippians 2:12-13 lets us know, *"Therefore, my beloved, as you have always obeyed, not as in my presence only, but now much more in my absence, work out your own salvation with fear and trembling; for it is God who works in you both to will and to do for His good pleasure.*" Don't take advantage of anything that God has done in your life whether big or small. Be thankful for all the things that He has done in your life and be thankful for who God is.

FILM STUDY

- Romans 8:10-20
- Romans 12:19
- 1 John 4:7-21
- Galatians 2:20
- Ephesians 1:13-14

Be thankful for the little things.

BE A STAR IN YOUR ROLE

Have you ever watched a sports game and heard a play-by-play announcer say during the game that a certain player is "a star in his or her role?" Within a team environment, there are many individuals with many God-given gifts. Every athlete on the team is assigned a role. In order for the team to succeed, each player must work hard and perform at a high level. Being assigned a role on any team requires a certain level of humility for an athlete to accept, especially when it is a lesser role. The main reason that it requires humility is because they were possibly the star of their previous team and have fewer opportunities to score in their new role.

Roles on a team include the coaches, star player/players, team captains, role players (the supporting cast), and bench players.

Coaches are incredibly important, they game plan and prepare for practices and games. Also, they encourage and constructively criticize. Coaches bring out the best of their teams while becoming leaders.

Star players are expected to lead by example and word. They are expected to perform and score at a high level. Team captains are expected to lead by example and word. They motivate the team before, during, and after games. Also, they encourage and constructively criticize their teammates to get the best out of them.

Role players do a solid job of doing other things. For example, defending, rebounding, passing, blocking, serving/spiking (volleyball), scoring when necessary, etc.

Bench players may not play as many minutes during games, but they will be asked cheer on teammates who typically play a considerable amount of time. They also play extremely hard in practice to help teammates prepare for games or matches. In addition, they must remain positive and be prepared to play in the game once the coaches call their number.

What does it mean for an athlete to be a star in his or her role? It means they are looking to reach their full potential by working hard to be the best that they can be regardless of their role. When each player on the team buys into their coaches' system and willingly sacrifices statistical success, awards, fame, fortune, etc. for the betterment of the team, the more success the team will have as a whole.

Similar to the team environment, this world has many Christians who possess God-given gifts meant to glorify God. We must make Christ's name known by preaching the Gospel of Jesus to unbelievers who do not know Him. There are many who are familiar with Jesus based on hearsay from others. They may say that they are Christians but don't live the way a Christian must live as instructed in the word of God. Others don't know who Jesus is because they were never presented The Good News, or maybe they didn't grow up in a Christian household.

In Matthew 28:19, before Jesus ascended into heaven, He told His disciples to *"Go and make disciples of all nations, baptizing them in the name of the Father and the Son and the Holy Spirit."* Like Jesus' disciples, we all have similar roles that consist of telling others about Jesus, making disciples, baptizing people, and using our respective God-given gifts to glorify Him. We can glorify God with our lives by first believing in Jesus Christ, living for God and being an example of Him everywhere we go by exhibiting the fruits of The Holy Spirit (Galatians 3:22-23). We can help those who are in need with the love of Christ. Motivate and encourage other Christians as they grow in their Christian walk. Grow in your walk with Jesus Christ and allow God to use you to be a star in your role as you become a disciple who makes disciples.

FILM STUDY

- Jeremiah 31:3
- Matthew 28:18-20
- Mark 16:15-16
- Luke 21:19
- John 17:26
- Hebrews 10:24
- 2 Corinthians 5:20
- Matthew 7:3-5
- Romans 12:1-2
- Galatians 6:1-3

Accept and be a star in your role.

THE GRIND NEVER STOPS

During "The Last Dance," a documentary highlighting Michael Jordan and the Chicago Bulls' 1997-98 season, Tim Grover (Jordan's former trainer) recalled a moment following Game 6 of the 1995 Eastern Conference Semifinals as the Orlando Magic defeated the Chicago Bulls. That night after the game, Grover said, "After the season, usually there is a time period where Michael takes some time off." Later he said to Jordan, "Michael, I'm about to get out of here. Let me know when you want me to see you [to train]." Jordan replied, "I'll see you tomorrow." Tim Grover added, "Michael had an obligation to himself, the fans, his teammates, the organization, his family, everybody." He recalled Jordan saying, "If you are going to sit down and take three hours out of your day to watch me on TV, I have an obligation to give you my best all the time."

By the way, the Bulls began the 1995-1996 season on a mission winning the first 23 out of 25 games and finished the season with an NBA record, 72-10. They ultimately went to the NBA Finals and won the NBA Championship vs. the Seattle Supersonics. Michael Jordan was named Finals MVP, averaging 27.3 points per game. After losing in the 1995 NBA Eastern Conference Semi-Finals vs. the Magic, the Chicago Bulls could have rested on their laurels particularly after winning three championships from 1991-1993. In addition, Jordan could have easily made an excuse of being rusty following his return to the starting lineup after his hiatus to play baseball. Due to Jordan and the Bulls' work ethic and their willingness to improve their overall games during the summer after the 1995 Semi-Final's loss, they were able to successfully prepare heading into the 1996 season. As a result of their preparation, the Chicago Bulls dominated and won at a high level.

In the "honeymoon" stage, many new believers are extremely excited and have a tremendous zeal to learn about the Christian faith. They get baptized, they separate themselves from old friends who don't necessarily have their best interests at heart and they ultimately begin to change the way they speak, think, and view things in general. This shows that the Holy Spirit is in their lives). In addition, they go to church and even pray and study the Bible. But as they move forward in life, they allow certain areas of life (work, family, fame, fortune, extracurricular activities, etc.) to distract them from constantly growing in the faith. As a result, they begin to have less zeal. They're not in the Word of God as much. They forget to pray and they fall into old habits that they displayed before they got saved. In times like these, God will have to allow those who reject or abandon Him to go through certain trials and tribulations so that they can recognize their need for Him. Always know that God wants to be glorified.

When we fail to seek God, good fruit will not be produced in our lives. One thing that we must understand is that the Christian walk doesn't end with our belief in Jesus Christ. It starts there. Christianity is not only a religion, it is a relationship between a person and God. Christian means "Christ-like." Life is a journey that presents ups and downs but by the grace of God, we have the Holy Spirit who is able to lead and guide us daily while giving us a peace that many will not understand (Philippians 4:7).

Similar to courting someone, you cannot expect to get know the other person unless you communicate with them and understand what they like or dislike, their past relationships, what makes them ticked, etc. God wants us to have a close, intimate relationship with Him, not only because He loves us but also because He desires us to be more like Jesus.

We grow in our relationship with God through constant communication with Him in prayer and as we read and study the Bible. In addition, we must always remember to center ourselves around like-minded individuals who have God as the foundation of their lives. They can hold us accountable and bring the best out of us. We cannot afford to rest on our laurels and be stagnant in our Christian walk as believers of Jesus Christ even if we have been Christians for 10, 20, 30, or 40 years. We should never feel like we have arrived just because we are Christians. We must always walk in humility, recognizing that we are imperfect individuals in need of a Savior who can perfect us daily. The more that we recognize our need for God, the more zeal we will possess to seek Him. The more zeal that we possess to seek God, the more that the Holy Spirit will produce the fruit of the Spirit within us (love, peace, joy, goodness, patience, kindness, faithfulness, gentleness, self-control). As the Holy Spirit produces fruit within us, the more we demonstrate the characteristics of Jesus Christ in the world around us and ultimately preach the Gospel. If you make a mistake in life, repent of your sins and move forward living the life that God has called you to live. Always remember to allow the Holy Spirit to lead and guide you each day. Don't rest on your laurels. Live a repentant life and watch what God will do for you.

FILM STUDY

- Philippians 3:12-20
  - John 15:5
  - John 16:13
- Galatians 5:22-23
  - Galatians 6:1-3

We can grow in our relationship with God.

ABOUT THE AUTHOR

 Travis Wilson hails from Salisbury, North Carolina. A 2011 graduate of Liberty University, Wilson majored in Sport Management. During his time at Liberty, he played three years of intramural basketball. He also served professionally as Assistant Girls Basketball Coach for Trinity Academy of Raleigh in Raleigh, North Carolina. Over the years, Wilson has matured and surrendered to a call to ministry. For years, he says he ran from this calling because of the challenges he witnessed his father facing as a preacher of the gospel of Jesus Christ. However, he came to realize the value in serving in this capacity despite the obstacles. After experiencing a life full of ups and downs, he came to recognize an undeniable desire to honor, glorify, and obey God in ministry. Now, his goal every day is to make a positive impact for God's glory in the lives of the next generation of believers.

Travis Wilson is available for speaking engagements and book club events. You can reach him via email: **tawilson2324@yahoo.com**.

CPSIA information can be obtained
at www.ICGtesting.com
Printed in the USA
LVHW011608301021
701978LV00020B/1179